Puerto Rico: Island of Promise

OTHER BOOKS BY RUTH GRUBER

Israel Today
Israel Without Tears
Destination Palestine

PUERTO RICO

Island of Promise

By RUTH GRUBER

HILL and WANG · NEW YORK

Copyright © 1960 by Ruth Gruber
Library of Congress Catalog Card Number: 60-10517
Manufactured in the United States of America

Preface

In the spring of 1958, I traveled to Puerto Rico to write a series of articles for the *New York Herald Tribune*. Nine years had elapsed since my first trip to the island to cover the historic inauguration of Governor Luis Muñoz Marín as the first elected governor of the island. In less than a decade the face of the island had changed.

The people were wiping out slums, flinging up new industries, building homes, schools, roads, luxurious hotels. Tourists were pouring in from the mainland, discovering the beauty of Puerto Rico and the warmth of its people. Thousands of visitors from underdeveloped countries around the world, women in golden saris, men in burnooses or African dress, were journeying to the island in the Caribbean to find out how their countries too could fight hunger and disease and begin their own Operation Bootstrap.

A year later my publishers, Lawrence Hill and Arthur Wang, two young, creative and (now, in retrospect, fortunately) slave-driving men, asked if I would expand the series of articles into a book. I agreed, and in the summer and fall of 1959 embarked on a voyage of discovery and rediscovery.

For I had old ties to the island. I had met my husband Phil Michaels in Puerto Rico. He, too, a native New Yorker, a member of the "Mayor's Advisory Committee on Puerto Ricans in New York," had been invited to Governor Muñoz' inauguration in gratitude for his work in helping the Puerto Ricans adjust to a new life. Our two children, Celia and David, though not Puerto Ricans, are our constant awareness of what Puerto Rico has meant for us.

This book was written with their help, as they taught me to see the island through their uncluttered honesty and their quick humor.

A list of the people in Puerto Rico and in the States who helped in gathering the material, in checking its accuracy, in letting us interview them for long hours at a time, in turning *mi casa es su casa*—my house is your house—into a daily reality, would fill pages of fine type. But there are some, not mentioned in the chapters of this book, whose counsel, criticism, suggestions, and hard work went far beyond the call of friendship or duty, and these I am listing here: Jesús M. Benítez, Clara Blumenthal, Katherine Bregman, Selma Buchwald, Gilbert Crandall and Ted Levine of the Economic Development Administration, Dr. Harry Gruber, Dan Levin, Lucy Pagán, and the men and women in the highly efficient Puerto Rico News Service.

And, as always, my gratitude to the editors of the *New York Herald Tribune* for giving me the opportunity to discover Puerto Rico and to use the material which first appeared in their pages.

ACKNOWLEDGMENTS

For the photographs reproduced here by permission the author extends thanks to Michel Alexis for the pictures on pages 4, 56, 59, 63, 65, 85, 91, 147, 162, 163, 166, 172, and 213; Andreu, page 135; Casa del Libro, Old San Juan, page 169; Roberto Cole, page 73; Commonwealth of Puerto Rico: Dept. of Agriculture and Commerce, pages 33 and 126; Dept. of Education, pages 133 and 139; Dept. of Labor, page 97; Dept. of State, pages 209 and 211; Div. of Community Education, page 199; Housing Authority, page 105; Office of the Governor, page 116; Planning Board, pages 21 and 25; Social Programs Administration, page 119. Also Frank Comandella, page 183; Jack Delano, pages 11, 88, 95, 107, 141, 154, and 155; Bernard A. Einson, pages 117, 181, and 194; *El Mundo* (San Juan), page 157; Elliott Erwitt, page 151; Fire Department, Utuado, page 137; Institute of Culture, Old San Juan, page 165; Richard Meek, page 9; Office of the Mayor of San Juan, page 102; Ed Rosskam, pages 35 and 203; Puerto Rico News Service, pages 5, 8, 10, 18, 19, 41, 43, 53, 104, 125, 128, and 175; Harold Underhill, page 189; University of Puerto Rico, page 143; and Hamilton Wright, page 7. The photographs on pages 37, 39, 51, 99, 101, 113, 121, and 131 were taken by the author.

The map on pages 28–29 is by Charles Kavenagh, *New York Herald Tribune;* and the map on page 60 is by Jack Luboff, *New York Herald Tribune.*

The photographs on the jacket of the cloth-bound edition and the cover of the paperback edition are used with the courtesy of the Commonwealth of Puerto Rico.

Contents

Puerto Rico: Island of Promise

CHAPTER 1

From San Juan to the Hills

It was 5:30 of an afternoon in Puerto Rico. A little group of Puerto Ricans and mainlanders drove through old San Juan on their way to the hills, to celebrate the hundredth anniversary in July 1959 of the birth of Luis Muñoz Rivera, the George Washington of Puerto Rico.

San Juan, a noisy, bustling metropolis on the north corner of the island, sprawled along the Atlantic Ocean, 1,600 miles southeast of New York. The afternoon sun threw stabs of silver in the wide blue bay. Hundreds of cars, bumper to bumper, were headed homeward. Queues of women, dressed in neat, starched cotton clothes, waited patiently at the bus stops to push their way on to the already overcrowded buses. In Padin's and the New York Department store, shoppers, preparing for the week end, were making their last-minute purchases of men's suits and airplane luggage, irregular shorts, costume jewelry, plastic wallets, artificial flowers, nylon stockings, and bright orange life jackets.

Thrifty Puerto Rican housewives were pushing carts of frozen foods and rice and beans through the bright fluorescent-lighted supermarkets. Teen-age girls in bright blouses and gay jumpers whose colors denoted their schools strolled happily together swinging their books, and singing Latin-American cha-cha songs. The

Aerial view of Old San Juan, with La Fortaleza,
the Governor's palace, in the foreground

tourists at the Caribe-Hilton were taking a final swim in the kidney-
shaped pool before they dressed for cocktails, dinner, and the
gambling casino.

A patient passenger driving at a snail's pace in this homeward
hour, could get a Cook's tour of old San Juan—the narrow crowded
streets, the old Spanish fortresses, the incredible number of shoe
stores, the tourist shops with their array of bongo drums, flam-
boyantly painted skirts, and off-the-shoulder rumba blouses. Music
came pouring out of the restaurants. Vendors on the street were
hawking bananas with picturesque names—finger bananas, apple
bananas, regular bananas, and dark green plantains.

As the quiet hour descended on the Bay of San Juan, the working day ended in the government buildings and in La Fortaleza, the
fortress palace of the Governor. Wives of some of the government
officials came with their children to drive their husbands home. The
slim-waisted daughter of the Secretary of State ran up the stairs to
use her daddy's typewriter to do her homework. The secretaries
went home.

Old San Juan (upper left) linked by the bridge Puente Dos
Hermanos to the Condado section (foreground)

In the last warm rays of sunlight the white Capitol with its dome
modeled after the Capitol building in Washington stood out above
the city. The Vice-President of the House, carrying a brief case
under his arm, walked swiftly down its majestic marble stairs to
take the bus home. Dr. Concepción de Gracia, the leader of the
PIP—*Partido Independentista Puertorriqueño* or Independence
Party—came out of his basement office into his waiting car.

Men were beginning to assemble in the Plaza de Armas, in front
of the City Hall, to sit or stand and watch the outdoor television
sets. Others were sitting on the stone benches, heatedly discussing
politics. In the pink, jewel-like Tapia Theatre on the far side of the
Plaza Colón—Colón is Spanish for Columbus—light-opera singers
were rehearsing a musical comedy imported from Spain.

Now, as you left old San Juan, you traveled slowly on broad,
wide streets built for twentieth-century traffic, past the quiet green
of Luis Muñoz Rivera Park named for the beloved leader, and the
airy glass-walled Supreme Court, inaugurated by United States
Chief Justice Earl Warren in 1956.

The hotels were beginning to turn on amethyst-green lights below their palm trees, giving the earth an eerie tropical glamour. Across a long white bridge, the Puente Dos Hermanos, you drove leisurely down the narrow neck of the Condado section between the blue-green ocean and the blue-green Condado lagoon, past some of the most beautiful homes on the island and the most expensive real estate, past the beautiful Spanish-tiled Condado Beach Hotel and the new La Concha Hotel, designed by Puerto Rican architects with a night club shaped like its name into an airy conch shell, where tonight Ruth Fernández, Puerto Rico's native daughter, would be singing joyously of the beauties of a sun-tanned skin, *"Yo soy mulata"* and, with her husband, would bring the house down in an English-Spanish drunk act, "We Puerto Ricans get drunk in any language."

San Juan was a city bursting at the seams. It had already swallowed Santurce, Hato Rey, and even Río Piedras, seven and a half miles away. From the Condado section, you drove into the main artery named for the first and most famous governor of the island, Ponce de León Avenue. This was the Broadway of Santurce, the heart of the shopping district. Chain stores from the States were rapidly opening branches—Pueblo Supermarkets owned by three young brothers from New Jersey, National Bellas Hess, the Franklin stores, running fierce and healthy competition with the stores that had first opened in old San Juan and now had branches here.

At Stop 18—San Juan is divided into "stops," a relic of the old trolley-car days before some of the streets had names—the lights were lit on the marquees of the Metro movie house showing "Tunnel of Love." Other movie theatres were playing Spanish-language films made in Spain and Mexico. The cabarets, respectable and otherwise, were getting ready for their nightly trade. El Calypso, a huge barn-like night club, was featuring a steel band from the Virgin Islands.

You drove past tall air-conditioned apartment buildings called "condominiums" where privately owned apartments sell from $25,000 to $50,000 for four or five rooms. San Juan was booming and you felt it everywhere. Real estate values had skyrocketed in three or four years. Houses that were worth $10,000 in 1955 were now worth $20,000 or $25,000. Land was so scarce and so valu-

El Fanguito (The Little Mud-hole), one of the worst
slums in San Juan, as it looked in the 1940's

able that pessimists predicted in ten years there would not be a tree
left standing in San Juan.

It was nearly six o'clock. The traffic was easing a little. The roads
were wider. The houses now were brightly painted, middle-class
houses with grilled doors and porches and garages. The middle
class was moving from old San Juan and from Santurce to the new
developments named Hyde Park, Los Angeles, San Francisco,
Eleanor Roosevelt, Truman, Beverly Hills, Garden Hills, Santa
María, Caparra Terrace, Villa Las Lomas, Summit Hill. Here lived
the white-collar workers from the new factories, the plant supervisors and managers from the States, the graduates of the University
of Puerto Rico—doctors, lawyers, architects, engineers. Many had
made the journey in ten years out of the dreadful slums of El
Fanguito (The Little Mud-hole) and La Perla (The Pearl) into the
low-cost housing projects of San José and Luis Llorens Torres, and
now into bright one-storied homes of their own.

Twenty years ago, the face of San Juan was the face of the very
rich, who were few, and the very poor, who were legion. There was
a small middle class which was old, mellow, and aristocratic. The

Luis Llorens Torres, low-cost housing project
facing the Atlantic Ocean, San Juan

city had beauty and wealth in a few sections, and poverty and
hunger nearly everywhere else. The slums were shocking hell-holes.
Children were naked, their bellies bloated with hunger. Women,
dressed in rags, nursed their babies on the streets. Men were unemployed and hungry. The houses were of tin and tar, or wood
gnawed away by termites. Garbage and sewage ran in little rivers
through the slums. The streets were planks laid across the foul-
smelling streams.

Twenty years later the slums were still there, but they were
shrunken in size. The people were being relocated into the low-cost
housing projects. Streets were being ripped up and new sewage
pipes laid. Urban renewal was a reality; some of the people were
renewing their own shacks, building concrete fronts and new outside walls after work.

The Dorado Beach Hotel where President Dwight D. Eisenhower played
golf during his historic Latin American tour in March 1960

In twenty years there had been a revolution in Puerto Rico, a
peaceful, sunny revolution that had changed the face of San Juan
and its people. The very rich still lived here and the very poor; and
now, since 1950, there was a substantial middle class too.

We were on our way to Barranquitas, the mountain village in the
interior some forty miles southwest of San Juan, to celebrate the
hundredth anniversary of the birth of the present governor's father,
Luis Muñoz Rivera, who lived from 1859 to 1916. The country
grew wilder as the road, in dizzy hairpin curves, climbed the mountains. Banana trees with huge jungle-like leaves, a great cluster of
bananas and their large wine-red flower hanging from each tree,
stood dense and mysterious along the mountain roads. Tobacco
fields were planted in contours, green and lush.

A supermarket in San Juan

The jíbaros—the country people—stood in front of their one-room wooden shacks, on the side of the road. In the tiny communities which had electricity, television antennas stood out in the evening sky. People sat inside the open doorways watching the little screens, wearing shawls against the evening mountain air. In the few darkened houses where there was still no electricity, the jíbaro families sat quietly on little front porches in the midst of scarlet birds-of-paradise, giant ferns, and the wax-like yellow trumpets of the *canario,* or canary flower.

Tomorrow at Barranquitas there would be a huge fiesta with Governor Luis Muñoz Marín, his wife, Doña Inés, the mayoress of San Juan, and people from the whole island making a pilgrimage to the little mountain town where Muñoz Rivera was born. Hundreds of beautiful wreaths of flowers would be carried across the island from nearly every community and laid on his grave. There would be speeches from the balcony of the City Hall and thousands

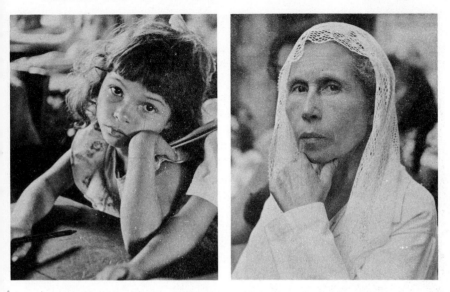

(Left) A schoolgirl in Sabana Seca, and (right) a woman participant
in the procession on San Juan's patron saint's day, June 24

of people, crowded tightly in the plaza, would fan themselves
against the blaze of noon, listening to the politicians speaking,
interrupting, laughing, applauding.

Now as night fell we were driving through mountain communities
that looked hundreds of years old. The island, one hundred miles
long and thirty-five miles wide, was ringed with beaches; the
Atlantic Ocean on its north, the Caribbean on its south, and green
forested mountains in its interior, peopled with tiny villages.

In one twilight hour we had driven across the two faces of Puerto
Rico. For there is San Juan and there are the hills. There is the
swift progress of the city and the immemorial way of life in the
mountains. And there are the men and women of vision trying to
bring about a victory for San Juan without making it a defeat for
the hills.

A peaceful revolution is sweeping the island. It is in Ponce, on
the southern coast, the second largest city, once a quiet Spanish
town, now bustling with factories and supermarkets. It is in Maya-

güez, the third largest city, lying on the western tip where the Caribbean Sea and the Atlantic Ocean meet, a tree-lined city awakening from a long sleep, as ships pull into its harbor carrying tuna from Peru and Africa to be sliced and canned, and then marketed around the world.

The peaceful revolution is in the small towns like San Germán, south of Mayagüez, where tourists come to see Porta Coeli, believed to be the oldest church in the New World, and where now new industries are turning out sweaters and baseballs for twentieth-century children. It is in the little fishing village of La Parguera with its phosphorescent bay where on moonless nights you can watch fish making lighted paths as they swim through water teeming with phosphorescence. It is in the villages perched on the side of mountain roads. It is in the sugar cane plantations, the pineapple fields, the coffee and tobacco lands.

You see revolution, feel it, smell it, hear it, know it all over the island. It is a revolution with many faces. The jíbaros change their way of life not in a generation or a decade, but in the hour or two it takes them to walk barefoot from their thatched hut in the hills to the shining new factories on the side of the main road.

The family, the basis of life in Puerto Rico, is in upheaval. Women are leaving the home to take jobs in the new industries. The old Spanish traditions are beginning to bend before the onslaught of Americanization.

The pull in Puerto Rico is between the Spanish past and the American present. "When Spain was here, they were individualists," Luis A. Ferré, a millionaire industrialist in Ponce, told me. "They saw things as Don Quixote saw them. They were quixotic. When the Americans came, they were pragmatic. They worked in teams. They had a sense of social responsibility. We in Puerto Rico have had the best of those two worlds. Puerto Rico is a crossroads in the Caribbean of Anglo-Saxon and Spanish culture, as Athens was a crossroads, or Renaissance Italy, and like Israel today."

In less than a decade, Puerto Rico has managed one of the most exciting political revolutions in modern history. It has evolved a creative answer to some of the explosive problems troubling the world—wiping out colonialism, establishing democratic self-government. Puerto Rico is neither a territory, an island possession, a colony, nor a state. In Spanish it calls itself proudly *Estado Libre Asociado,* a Free Associated State. It is a Commonwealth within the American Union. It evolved this revolution without recourse to dictators, without shooting down its leaders, without building an army that might threaten at any moment to usurp power.

Yet Puerto Rico has by no means solved all her problems. There is agony and beauty on the island. There is ferment and stagnation as well as dynamism and creativity. For a quarter of a million of tourists a year, Puerto Rico is an island paradise. For Puerto Ricans, for too many Puerto Ricans, it is paradise unfulfilled. There is still too much hunger. The island still cannot feed 2,300,000 people, though it hopes by 1975 to have enough work for everyone. The birth rate is still explosive.

The way of life changes each year for the people of San Juan and the hills as more industries come down to the island, as more land is distributed to the landless, as more jobs are created, and more schools and hospitals are built. Puerto Rico is an island paradox, and the roots of that paradox lie deep in its past.

CHAPTER 2

The Hand of Spain

The hand of Spain lies everywhere on Puerto Rico. Columbus discovered the islands of the Caribbean for Spain's Ferdinand and Isabella. On his first voyage across the Sea of Darkness in his three little sailing vessels, the *Santa María,* the *Pinta,* and the *Niña,* with a crew made up in part of criminals pardoned for the mad adventure, Columbus set foot in the New World on an island he described in his diary as "so green that it is a pleasure to look upon it." He called it San Salvador, in honor of the Holy Saviour. Its Indian name was Guanahaní, an island in the Bahamas southeast of Florida.

A year later he returned to the Caribbean, became the first island-hopper, and on November 19, 1493, discovered Puerto Rico. This time the Great Admiral, now a hero in Spain, sailed with a fleet of seventeen vessels and fifteen hundred men. Young noblemen begged to go along, dreaming of the jewels and gold they would find in the West Indies. Columbus took horses and cattle, seeds, and vines, to colonize the Caribbean.

No one knows where he dropped anchor in Puerto Rico. There are almost as many towns, I discovered, which claim Columbus as there are farmhouses in the United States where George Washington is supposed to have slept. Aguada and Aguadilla, twin towns

Parting of Columbus from Ferdinand and Isabella

on the northwest coast, which seem to have the best claim, are still feuding. Ponce claims him. So do Mayagüez and Cabo Rojo. Even his son Ferdinand helps confuse history by saying his fleet landed on the west side of the island, but they found Indian houses and a plaza on the east side.

Columbus, who named most of the islands after saints, named this one San Juan Bautista, St. John the Baptist. But down the centuries people began to call the island by the name of its most important harbor, Puerto Rico, the rich port. The Indians called their island *Borinquen*, a name still affectionately used for both the island and its people. Even the national anthem is called *"La Borinqueña."*

Although Columbus discovered Borinquen, it was a young Spanish officer traveling with him who had the greatest influence in its development. For he fell in love with the island's beauty and came back fifteen years later, in 1508, to become its Spanish governor. That man was Juan Ponce de León.

Ponce, with his helmet, armor and breastplate, was every inch a *conquistador* to the almost naked Indians. There were some thirty thousand Arawak Indians and a sprinkling of their historic enemies, the fierce Caribs, living then on the island. The Arawaks were peace-loving, gentle Indians who farmed the green semitropical island. They lived together in large villages with a strong central government controlled by a *cacique,* a chief or king. The Indians had six or seven wives who worked the fields while the men hunted and fished. Though to some of the more predatory Spaniards they seemed simple and primitive, their culture was relatively advanced and their stone sculpture ranks among the finest found in the New World. They were apparently much like the gentle Taino Indians of Española (later called Hispaniola, and then divided by France and Spain into Haiti and the Dominican Republic) whom Columbus described as "such an affectionate and generous people, and so tractable, that I assure your Highnesses there are no better people or land in the world. They love their neighbors as themselves, and their speech is the sweetest and the gentlest in the world, and they always speak with a smile."

The fate of these people who loved their neighbors as themselves was sealed soon after the Spaniards colonized Puerto Rico. By 1511, three years after Ponce became governor, the pattern of colonialism, which was to plague the island in different forms for four hundred years, was set by law. The Arawaks were distributed among the loyal soldiers of His Majesty, King Ferdinand. Under

Columbus landing at Hispaniola (Haiti and Dominican Republic)

the Spanish system of *encomiendas,* the island was divided among
the Spaniards; the Indians were distributed among the conquerors
to do their work. In exchange, the peaceful Arawaks were to be
protected from their enemies, the Caribs, and taken into the Mother
Church.

The Great Seal of Puerto Rico granted to the island in the early
days of the colonization by Ferdinand and Isabella

Ponce was an able administrator. Unlike many Spanish conquerors, he did not conceive of Spain's role in her West Indian
colonies as one of conquering and decimating the Indians. His was
a live-and-let-live philosophy within the framework of sixteenth-
century colonialism. When there was no conflict of interests, he
even adopted some of their customs. The Indians exchanged names
as a token of friendship; Ponce de León traveled around Borinquen
giving his name to hospitable Indian chiefs and taking theirs. In

Juan Ponce de León

gratitude, the Chief of the South, Agueybana, gave Ponce one of his wives as a gift for a Spanish nobleman.

A number of the Spaniards, falling in love with the island, sent back for their wives and children. Ponce led the way; he built a stone cottage for his wife Inéz, their three little daughters, and only son, in Caparra, the second oldest city in the New World. Life for Inéz and the children was not easy. Caparra is now less than a twenty-minute drive from the center of San Juan; at that time it was an almost inaccessible swamp land, infested with mosquitoes.

There was a plague of huge ants that overran the houses of the Spanish settlers and the native Indians. Ponce and his men devised the technique, now common in any insect-ridden country, of putting the posters of their beds as well as the legs of their tables and chairs in cans of water. Later his family moved to the harbor where life was more comfortable.

But Ponce de León became a victim of Spanish intrigue, lost his job as governor, and in 1513 left Puerto Rico with three small ships. He had heard legends from the Indians about a magic spring that cured rheumatism and made people young again. Ponce sailed north looking for the Fountain of Youth and discovered Florida.

Puerto Rican wits tell you that Ponce was the first Puerto Rican migrant to the States. In 1521, old and probably rheumatic, he returned to Florida, was wounded by an Indian arrow, and with a handful of survivors sailed to Cuba, where he died. In 1559, his grandson brought his bones back to Puerto Rico and they now lie behind a white marble slab in the Cathedral of San Juan Bautista in old San Juan.

The Spaniards conquered the Indians physically and morally, forcing them to pan the rivers for gold and farm the land, taking their women as concubines and occasionally as wives. But in a time-honored manner, the Indians in part conquered their conquerors. Long after the Arawaks were wiped out, the Spaniards achieved status by imitating them.

In the sixteenth century, the Indians lay in hammocks, fanning themselves with palm leaves, inhaling tobacco through their nostrils with a primitively shaped pipe. In the eighteenth century, it was the mark of nobility for a Spanish lady to lie in a hammock, fan herself, and smoke a cigar.

Words are a clue to the civilization which created them. Many of the words which the Spaniards heard for the first time from the Indians and passed on to the rest of the world point up the Indian culture which the conquerors adopted. Tobacco came from the Indian word *tabaco;* hammock was the Indian word *hamac;* canoe was an Indian boat; hurricane came from the Indian *Huracan,* an Indian god of evil and tempests.

From the earliest Spanish days, Puerto Rico had two profiles:

A street in Spanish colonial San Juan about 1550; total population 500

there was the city and there were the hills. There was San Juan and there was the hinterland. There were the *conquistadores,* the Spanish settlers, the soldiers, the nobility living in the city; and there were the people in the hills.

Under the Spaniards San Juan became a walled fortress. In 1533 the city began building the famous fort La Fortaleza where now the governor lives, to guard itself against attacks. In 1586 a permanent garrison was installed at El Morro on the northwest tip, to protect the city from invasion by sea. But the rest of the island with its harbors and soft trade winds became a paradise for pirates, slave traders and buccaneers. They anchored in hidden coves around the island; they traded with the settlers and the Indians, buying food and supplies with pirate gold. Some stayed when they found they could live easily off the land.

Captain Kidd himself, who had a wife and children in New York, sailed his black-flagged ship through the West Indies at the turn of the seventeenth century. He gave a bad name to the "honest" pirates who at least paid for their food. Kidd was a cheat. He got the natives to bring food aboard his ship and then put them ashore without pay while he cavalierly sailed off for new loot.

Wherever you go on the island, but especially in Ponce, you hear stories that Captain Kidd buried some of his treasure there, that the little island off Ponce called "Caja de Muertos"—Dead Men's Chest, was Robert Louis Stevenson's model for *Treasure Island*. Even the ship on which young Jim Hawkins sailed with "some of the wickedest men that God ever allowed upon the sea" was called *Hispaniola*.

For centuries, Puerto Rico's strategic location helped write the island's history. Before the Spaniards came, it was a stepping-stone for the Indians in their wars against each other. For Spain, it served as a strategic link to her colonies in the New World. For America in the twentieth century, it was to become a bridge between North and South America as well as a base for troops poised to protect the Panama Canal.

The expanding nations of the sixteenth century, England, France, Denmark, Holland, seeking footholds in the New World, sought to capture Puerto Rico. The Dutch burned part of San Juan in 1625. But it was England that eyed the island most hungrily. England was already in the Antilles. If she could control Puerto Rico, she could control the trade routes to the West Indies. She could defend her other islands and take the offensive in trade and territorial expansion. The oceans were highways and Puerto Rico was a natural stopover. In 1595 Sir Francis Drake attacked the island and was driven back; in 1598 the Earl of Cumberland occupied it for five months. He was driven off by an epidemic.

The British, who had defeated the great Spanish Armada in a week's fighting in the English Channel in 1588, failed to conquer the tiny outpost of empire to which the Spaniards clung tenaciously. Yet they continued to pound at the island's defenses. In 1729, two years after England and Spain were again at each other's throats, the British Governor of the Leeward Islands, John Hart, once again suggested to the British that they ought to capture Puerto Rico. In a letter to the Lord President of the Council of Trade and Plantations, he explained why Puerto Rico's strategic location would be valuable to the British: "It is a very fertile island, well water'd and capable of producing everything that grows both in the Islands and Continent of America."

What Puerto Rico looked like in the eighteenth century is described by an English sailor in a fascinating manuscript now in the Library of Congress called *"Journal of a Captive. Remarkable Occurrences from the year 1745 to 1748, during the far greater part of which times I was a prisoner in the hands of the French and Spaniards; transcribed from my private notes in Rhode Island. Anno 1748."* The author, believed to be John George, declared:

"It is one of the finest islands I ever saw, and I verily believe not any one island in the West Indies is more capable of improvement than this; but through the pride and sloth of the inhabitants it is the far greater part of it still a wilderness. It abounds in oranges, lemons, citrons, limes, etc., in such plenty that they are not worth the gathering. There are prodigious quantities of bananas, plantens, coco nutts, pine apples, mountain cabbage; with a great many other fruits and vegetables. . . . In short, there is not any thing for the support of human nature but may here be found or cultivated. It might in the hands of the English or Dutch be rendered a paradise on earth, but the present inhabitants are mere devils."

The people whom the captive sailor was describing were no longer the native Indians. They had been virtually wiped out by the white man's diseases and as a result of overwork. He was apparently talking of the pirates and settlers who had fled to the island from the British Caribbean colonies and had intermarried with Negro slaves.

The slave traffic began as early as 1511, when the Spaniards brought the first Negroes from Africa to Puerto Rico. In fewer than thirty years, from 1526 to 1553, they landed about 15,000 African slaves on the island. For three hundred years the traffic in slaves continued, with African blood mixing freely with Spanish blood and what was left of Indian blood.

Few settlers came to the island in the sixteenth and seventeenth centuries; the gold had run out and the lure of gold in Mexico and Peru became so attractive to the Spaniards in Puerto Rico that in order to keep its population, the governor threw into jail anyone who tried to emigrate from Puerto Rico.

Strategically Puerto Rico continued to be regarded as important as Gibraltar. Throughout the eighteenth century, it was a pawn in the Anglo-Spanish chess game in the Caribbean. Indeed, British envoys talked of trading Gibraltar for Puerto Rico. But the Spaniards would not relinquish the little island which lay astride Britain's trade routes. On February 17, 1797, British Lieutenant General Sir Ralph Abercromby, after capturing Trinidad, attacked San Juan. But by now the Spaniards had built excellent fortifications; and Abercromby was trounced by the Spanish troops, the native militia, and Puerto Rico's peasants who came down from the hills to fight with the people of the city.

The people of Puerto Rico took new pride in their island, and their loyalty to Spain. Earlier they had helped the young Thirteen Colonies win their independence from England. Two American ships, the *Endawock* and the *Henry,* fleeing the *Glasgow,* a British frigate, took refuge in Mayagüez on August 1, 1777. The Puerto Ricans helped the young revolutionaries by raising the Spanish flag on the ships and granting them the right of asylum. The sovereignty of the United States was thus first recognized by the people of Puerto Rico.

In the late eighteenth and turbulent nineteenth century, with Spain in turmoil at home, her possessions captured or fighting for independence in the New World, Puerto Rico remained staunchly loyal to the motherland. She too, in the spirit of the times, wanted self-government, though not independence. She sought to get it by peaceful rather than by violent means.

In gratitude Spain allowed Puerto Rico to have one delegate in the Spanish Cortes. Don Ramón Power y Giralt, the island's first real leader, arrived in Spain in 1810 and made so strong an impression on the Spaniards that he was elected vice-president of that body. Don Ramón prevailed on the Cortes to abrogate the dictatorial powers it had given the Governor of Puerto Rico and to grant new legal procedures for civil rights. He urged the Spanish rulers to set up an independent *Intendencia* to promote industry and agriculture, and administer the royal treasury. He succeeded; and on November 28, 1811, Spain sent Alejandro Ramírez to Puerto Rico. His name is still honored on the island as one of the best administrators Spain sent in the last years of her reign in America.

Now trade with the United States began in earnest, and, under

Plaza de Armas, main square of San Juan, 1900

Ramírez, a royal *cédula* (decree) of August 10, 1815, opened the island as a haven of refuge. The Spaniards had first liberalized their attitude toward immigration in 1778. Now in the nineteenth century, immigrants brought new blood into the strategic outpost which the Spaniards had for centuries kept tightly closed to immigration or emigration.

Today Puerto Rico is thought of as an island of emigration—save for the hundreds of thousands of tourists discovering it anew. But under Ramírez' enlightened rule people began migrating *to* Puerto Rico to live. They were Catholics seeking a Catholic refuge. In 1816, 83 Americans came from Louisiana; in the wake of the Louisiana Purchase of 1803, they preferred Spanish-Catholic Puerto Rico to Protestant American rule. French families from Haiti, unhappy after the revolution of 1801 in which Toussaint l'Ouverture overthrew the French, migrated to the island. Wealthy loyalist families from Venezuela and Santo Domingo came seeking haven under the Spanish flag. From Philadelphia came Irish Catholics with red hair, white skin, and blue eyes. Their descendants who have inherited these features still live in the interior of the island near Castañer and Utuado. The population spurted from 155,000 in 1800 to 500,000 by the middle of the century and to 900,000 in 1898.

The bloodstreams of all these migrants fused to make the Puerto Rican of today. He is not a Negro, though 20% of the population is Negro. He is not an Indian yet the golden skin, the high cheekbones, the aquiline nose, the gentleness and hospitality of the Indians are a common trait all over the island. He is not a Spaniard yet he may have the blond hair of Northern Spain and the pure white skin of Barcelona.

The wave of reform that swept Europe in the nineteenth century reached the island that had for so long lain on the periphery of enlightenment, untouched by the industrial revolution. In 1868 a few hundred peasants captured the town hall of Lares and pronounced the birth of the Republic of Puerto Rico. But they were quickly suppressed and their leaders were sentenced to death.

But Spain itself was now in complete upheaval. Queen Isabella the Second was overthrown and Spain became a republic in 1873. Within a year the republic fell. The monarchy was reinstated and Puerto Rican efforts at reform met with new terror. Native leaders were thrown into jail without trial. There had never been freedom of religion or freedom of the press; now there was strict censorship and all public meetings were barred.

Out of the wave of reform arose leaders of the Puerto Rican people, intellectuals like Eugenio Maria de Hostos, Ramon Betances, Ruiz Belvis, and Luis Muñoz Rivera, the father of the present governor. In two sentences, de Hostos described the long history of Spanish colonization in the island: "About material resources there is nothing to be said; the colonial government has left us in economic misery. About moral resources there is nothing to rationalize: the colonial state has left us in a state of psychological misery."

CHAPTER 3

A Commonwealth Is Born

In "Arsenic and Old Lace," a comedy revived in San Juan in 1960, a beguiling lunatic brought the house down each time he burst forth, dressed to the teeth like Teddy Roosevelt, shouting to the audience to charge San Juan Hill.

The San Juan up which Teddy Roosevelt charged was in Cuba. But it was because of Cuba that the United States went to war with Spain in 1898 and incidentally captured Cuba's sister island, Puerto Rico.

Why did the United States take Puerto Rico? There seems to be a conspiracy of silence. Most books on the island leave the question intriguingly unanswered. Some say, in swift passing, that we took the island in order to protect the Panama Canal. The need for a canal to link America's east and west coasts was recognized; plans for building a Central American canal were well known. But negotiations for the Panama Canal were not started until 1903 and the first ship sailed through the Canal in 1914.

Others say that after the Puerto Rican coffee and sugar cane planters began to trade heavily with the United States, it was inevitable that Puerto Rico would become part of the United States. But Cuba, too, was trading with the United States. Puerto Rico was like one of the forgotten eggs that the Prophet Isaiah spoke of,

27

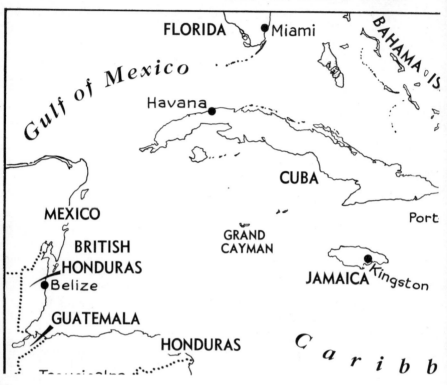

"and as one gathereth eggs that are left, have I gathered all the earth." We were gathering up earth, too. We were looking for new naval bases and colonies. We were taking up where Britain had left off, reviving our faith in Manifest Destiny. Henry Cabot Lodge wanted us to annex Canada, Cuba, and the Hawaiian Islands. William Randolph Hearst in the *New York Journal,* along with the publishers of the *Chicago Tribune* and the *Denver Republican,* discovered that stories about Spanish atrocities with pictures of Cuban rebels dying in concentration camps, sold newspapers.

Theodore Roosevelt, who was later to become a great reform president, was Assistant Secretary of the Navy in 1897. Exploiting the slogan then sweeping America, *"Cuba Libre"*—Free Cuba,

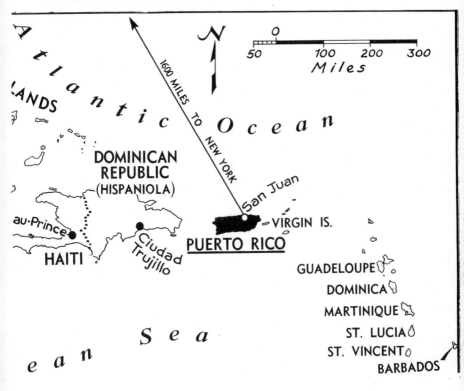

Roosevelt declared that "No triumph of peace is quite so great as the supreme triumphs of war."

"This country needs a war," he explained seriously, as though he were talking of a good five-cent cigar. War was for "the benefit done to our people by giving them something to think of which isn't material gain, and especially the benefit done our military forces by trying both the Army and Navy in actual practice."

A holiday air helped whip up the fervor for war with Spain. America's favorite song was "There'll Be A Hot Time In The Old Town Tonight." Roosevelt resigned from the Navy, gathered polo players, cowboys, and clubmen in a cavalry regiment called the "Rough Riders" and made his famous charge up San Juan Hill.

When the Spaniards surrendered on July 17, 1898, John Hay congratulated Theodore Roosevelt in a letter, "It has been a splendid little war."

Puerto Rico was captured at the end of the "splendid little war." On July 25, 1898, General Nelson A. Miles landed in Puerto Rico. Some observers on the island have suggested that he sailed to Puerto Rico because he was jealous of General William R. Shafter, the three-hundred-pound commander of the United States troops in Cuba; by capturing the island next to Cuba, he too could win immortality. But others point out that the island was part of the original war plan, interrupted by the bottling up of the American Navy in Santiago Bay in Cuba.

Finley Peter Dunne, the Will Rogers of his day, who called himself in his humorous columns and speeches "Mr. Dooley," described the musical-comedy character of General Miles's occupation of Puerto Rico as "Gin'ral Miles' Gran' Picnic and Moonlight Excursion."

Even the reception which the American troops received from the Puerto Ricans had a comic-opera flavor. In San Germán I heard the story of a Captain Rivera, who was in charge of a local garrison of about twenty men. As the Americans hove into sight, Captain Rivera gave an immortal command to his troops.

"If there are a lot of Americans, run. If there are a few, hide. If there are none, engage in battle."

There was almost no battle to engage in. Spain, already withering in Latin America, was struck a death blow.

The war ended with the Treaty of Paris in 1898. The United States annexed Puerto Rico in the Caribbean, and the Philippines and Guam in the Pacific. Cuba became a protectorate of the United States under the Platt Amendment, giving us the power to intervene at any time to preserve order and protect Cuba's independence. Over three decades later, in 1934, President Franklin Delano Roosevelt sought to repair the damage of the Platt Amendment by relinquishing it.

Teddy Roosevelt, by no means an evil man, had epitomized, in his own forceful creative personality, a stage in the growth of young America, an inevitable stage perhaps and one which we have now completely outgrown. It took the second Roosevelt—Franklin Delano—to mark the end of the age of adolescence and to launch us into maturity in the Good Neighbor Policy of his administration.

Beyond the intriguing question of why we took Puerto Rico, the solid fact emerges that the Puerto Ricans did not ask to become part of the United States. They were our spoil of war. After thirty years of neglect and indifference, the men of the New Deal, in agonizing reappraisal, made the country aware that we were as responsible for the Puerto Ricans as a parent is for the child who never asked to be born.

We had much to undo.

By one of those acts of irony in which history abounds, the Spaniards, barely a year before the Americans landed, gave Puerto Rico an *Autonomous Charter*. On November 25, 1897, Luis Muñoz Rivera succeeded in getting Praxedes Sagasta, Prime Minister of Spain, to grant Puerto Rico its first constitution and to give it self-government. Spain, after four hundred years of oppression, corruption, and bureaucracy, suddenly set the clock forward.

It was not too little but it was too late. The Spanish-American war intervened.

The United States, with almost no political experience in ruling colonies, promptly set the clock back. It withdrew the autonomy which the Puerto Ricans had wrested from Spain. For a year and a half, American military government ruled the island.

On April 12, 1900, Congress passed the Foraker Act; it was the first Organic Act for Puerto Rico, setting up the formula of civil government. The United States guaranteed that it would protect the island; it set up a *Cámara de Delegados,* a House of Representatives, to which the people were allowed to elect delegates. But home rule was abandoned. The United States now followed the colonial pattern by which the British had ruled the American colonies. The governor and almost every official of importance was appointed by the President of the United States. The President also appointed the members of the upper house of the Puerto Rican legislature. The Puerto Ricans were Americans, but they were not to become citizens of the United States until the Jones Act, the second Organic Act, was passed in 1917. Puerto Rico was still a colony, run, not from Madrid, but from Washington and New York.

Despite the political jingoism of the time, there were Americans who were both idealists and realists. The Foraker Act itself, though it was politically backward, contained economic reforms that were remarkably far-sighted. It continued the Spanish policy of exempting the people from paying any taxes to the Federal Government.

Many mainlanders, traveling to the island, are surprised to find that even today Puerto Ricans pay only an income tax to the Commonwealth of Puerto Rico but no federal tax; and that the Federal Government returns all the excise tax on rum to the Puerto Rican treasury, a sum which now amounts to $20,000,000 a year.

Land reform is the dream of most progressive governments in Latin America. But in 1900 the Foraker Act included the famous "500-Acre Law" to restrict corporations from buying up most of the arable land. Unfortunately there was no one interested in enforcing the law until forty years later.

America's idealism was to show itself in education and health. In Cuba, a group of army doctors, working with Major Walter Reed, gave their lives to find the breeding places of mosquitoes which caused yellow fever. In Puerto Rico, doctors were sent from the States to carry on Walter Reed's fight against yellow fever. Public health programs were started to teach the island people prevention of disease as well as cure. Under the Spaniards, there was education only for the elite. Puerto Rico had an "intelligentsia." But since the vast majority had no education at all, the United States sent teachers from the States. In 1903 the University of Puerto Rico was founded to help the island develop its own teaching force.

Still Puerto Rico was little more than a neglected child. Poverty beset the island. Sugar was king, a sick king. There were a few Puerto Rican sugar planters; but most of the crop was controlled by absentee owners in the States.

To many of Puerto Rico's intellectuals, the only answer seemed to be independence. Perhaps if Puerto Rico were independent it could work out its own destiny.

In the thirties the depression was racking America. Puerto Rico

Panoramic view of a rural community

was now tied to America with economic umbilical cords. There were no statistics; some said that more than 150,000 people were out of work and starving; others said there were many more. In the sugar fields the men worked for five months and then there was the "dead time." Women were paid four cents an hour in the needle industry. Babies died of dysentery and hunger. There was no birth control. There was only death control: only the fittest survived.

In New York's Greenwich Village, Luis Muñoz Marín, the young son of Puerto Rico's patriot, Luis Muñoz Rivera, talked to anyone who would listen, about the plight of his beloved island. In the early twenties Muñoz was a Socialist, influenced by Puerto Rico's Socialist leader Santiago Iglesias, the father of the labor movement there. Muñoz returned to Puerto Rico in 1926, gave up socialism, and joined the so-called Liberal Party. In 1932 he was elected Senator-at-large to the Puerto Rican Legislature and worked closely with Washington in organizing Puerto Rico's WPA project called the PRRA—the Puerto Rico Reconstruction Administration.

But in a few years Muñoz became anathema to the Liberal Party. He preached independence across the country and denounced the absentee sugar lords. In 1936 Muñoz, in Washington, wrote an independence bill which was introduced in Congress but died still-born in committee. A year later he was expelled by the Liberal Party and for a year went into political eclipse.

The next year, in July 1938, he created a new party, the Popular Democratic Party. It started with a handful of followers who, like Muñoz, had revolted against the Liberal Party. The slogan of the Popular Democratic Party was *"Pan, Tierra y Libertad"*—Bread, Land and Liberty. Its emblem was the *"pava,"* the straw hat worn by the jíbaros. The city slum dwellers, the jíbaros in their shacks in the hills, the poor Puerto Ricans rising against both the absentee owners and the handful of local millionaire families, the hungry and exploited everywhere rallied around the new party. Intellectuals and idealists joined them. Their battle cry was *"Vergüenza contra Dinero"*—dignity versus money.

Muñoz' strength came from the jíbaros. Poet, bohemian, rebel, philosopher, he went to the hills to live among the peasants. The jíbaros responded. Muñoz became their leader, and they in turn taught him their ancient wisdom. It was an old jíbaro back in the twenties, Muñoz' wife Doña Inés told me, who gave him what was to become the key to the campaign for the 1940 election. "Muñoz," the jíbaro pointed out, "the people are selling their votes."

The political parties were giving a two-dollar bribe to each person who voted. Sometimes they gave a man a pair of two-dollar shoes. Muñoz went up and down the island saying to the people, "Don't sell your vote. Lend it to me." This was the crux of his campaign. The vote became the symbol of democracy. If he could teach his people the power and sanctity of the vote, then he could teach them the greatest truth he knew—that strength lay within them, that the people themselves had the power to lift themselves up.

Traveling around the island, experiencing its hunger, he moved toward a new stage in his political development. The total inde-

(Left) A farm worker, Cidra and (right) a farm worker near Toa Baja

pendence that had seemed so attractive a few years ago now seemed to be no panacea at all. His people were hungry. Food was the answer.

He took the question of independence out of the campaign. "Status is not the issue now," he said. "Let's clothe the naked, feed the hungry, care for the sick before we worry about status."

He was beginning to talk to his friends unofficially of a still vague idea of autonomy within the American Union. But officially the campaign was for economic reform. It was a pro-United States election campaign. Muñoz, working closely with Franklin D. Roosevelt and Harold L. Ickes in whose Interior Department Puerto Rico was administered, had learned how much Puerto Rico needed the United States and how much a liberal administration in the United States could help the Puerto Ricans. Federal surveys studied 11,000 people on Puerto Rico's tiny island of Vieques off the east coast of the big island, working mainly in sugar. The total income for the 11,000 people was $500 per week. The PRERA, the Puerto Rican Emergency Relief Administration, set up by

Washington in 1938, spent a million dollars a month to feed the people of Puerto Rico. The days of Yankee imperialism were over. America's Manifest Destiny in the thirties was to care for the people of the island it had once conquered with flamboyant flag-waving. The depression had matured Americans; they had a new sense of responsibility toward the suffering people on their island outpost.

As election day, November 5, 1940, neared, the campaign went into high gear. The Popular Democratic Party, or Populares, which had started from nothing two years before, fired the imagination of the people. Horses were used to get to places that were inaccessible by car. Loud-speakers were placed on top of trucks and oxcarts. Muñoz would go to the top of a hill and through the loud-speaker make a speech that could be heard in the valleys. The opposition, the Liberal Party, and a coalition of Union Republicans and Social-ists, would rush a truck to another hill to make their rebuttal. In fifty days, using records that were played over and over again, Muñoz made 30,000 speeches.

The leaders of the Populares drafted twenty-two bills they hoped to put into effect if they were elected. Then they went around the island reading the bills to people who could not read.

It was essentially an agrarian campaign, to give land to the landless, to break up some of the vast sugar plantations that covered as much as ten and fifteen thousand acres each. One of the principal planks was a Puerto Rican Land Authority Bill to put teeth into the 500-Acre Law.

Some of the large sugar corporations began to see the handwrit-ing on the wall. On the day of election, a few of them tried to pre-vent their sugar cane workers from voting. Some of the managers locked their gates. Others swiftly organized fiestas with roast pigs and free-flowing rum to make the cane cutters forget to vote. But the people voted. Where the gates were closed, they piled into com-pany trucks; standing tightly against each other for support, they rammed through the gates and drove to the polls.

Legends grew up about that election day. There is the story of the blind man who came to the polls. Each party had its own watchers and all the watchers tried to help the blind man mark

Governor Luis Muñoz Marín being sworn in as the first elected governor.
Behind him is his appointed predecessor, the late Jesús T. Piñero

his ballot. "You don't have to help me," the blind man said. "I've been practicing. I put so many fingers across the paper and so many fingers down. That's where I put my cross to vote for Muñoz Marín."

At one of the polls, a crowd of people stood in line to vote. Everyone was in high spirits, chattering, arguing, laughing. Along came a man with brand-new shoes, taking his place in line. His shoes were so new they squeaked. The people stopped talking. In dead silence they fastened their eyes on his shoes. Everyone knew the shoes were the two-dollar bribe.

The victory of the two-year-old Popular Democratic Party against its combined opposition took everyone by surprise. Although the Party won by the slim majority of one in the Senate, Muñoz became President of the Senate and the unquestioned leader of Puerto Rico. His party had won 38% of the total vote; in the next election in 1944 they won 64% of the total vote. Today they control nearly every political office in the land.

The election of 1940 marked the beginning of the peaceful revolution. It was a revolution at the polls.

In 1941, Rexford Guy Tugwell was appointed governor of the island by President Roosevelt, and responsible to his good friend, the Secretary of the Interior, Harold L. Ickes. Puerto Rico became an outpost of the New Deal. Tugwell knew that there was justified resentment against many of the governors sent from Washington. He knew too that Muñoz, not he, was the leader of the people; that the people trusted Muñoz as they would never trust him, an outsider and a "continental." But the two men, working together, could put through reforms that the New Dealers had only dreamt of in Washington. Together they worked out the techniques of the Puerto Rican revolution. They created the Planning Board. They strengthened the Civil Service. They created the Transportation Authority, they reorganized the Water Resources Authority for cheap electricity, they set up a Housing Authority to wipe out the slum-holes of the cities. They attracted a group of young idealists and intellectuals who are still the leaders today.

The quiet Eastern college professor had first gone to Puerto Rico to study the land problem in March 1934. It is a place, he wrote in *The Stricken Land,* "where starvation ensued upon cruelty to the land." Now as governor, he was able to put through agricultural and social reforms that made some members of Congress in Washington see red. The newspapers of Puerto Rico opposed Tugwell but the people of Puerto Rico backed him. And their leaders, eager for reform, recognized his idealism. He was the intellectual who had come out of an ivory tower to become the most effective continental governor the island had ever known.

But his enemies in Washington finally made his position almost untenable. Tugwell, understood in Puerto Rico and misunderstood in Washington, resigned as governor in 1946. To replace him, President Harry S. Truman appointed the first Puerto Rican as governor, the late Jesús Piñero, an outstanding man who had been

Inauguration parade in San Juan, January 2, 1949

the elected Resident Commissioner in Washington and had worked closely with Muñoz in the Popular Party.

Piñero was one of the early leaders who had gone into the hills to educate the people. He took movies and traveled around the island, projecting the pictures on cement walls to show them to the jíbaros.

In Washington, Piñero spent much of his time in the Department of Interior where I was then Special Assistant to Secretary Ickes, working on Alaska. Piñero would ruefully bemoan the fact that our problems were diametrically opposite: Puerto Rico had too many people and too little land; Alaska had no people and a vast land one fifth the size of the United States. If only there were some way, he would shake his head, of solving the problems of both territories at once.

On August 5, 1947, President Truman and the Congress of the United States gave the people of Puerto Rico greater self-government than they had ever known. They were to elect their own governor. It was the first political reform on the island since the Jones Act of 1917 had made them citizens. Elections were held on November 2, 1948, and Muñoz was swept into power, the first elected governor in island history.

Only the Puerto Ricans could have turned the inauguration of their governor into a combination of Thanksgiving, a bloodless revolution, and a week-long fiesta that outdid any Polish wedding. There were huge balls every night. There were tours of the island for invited celebrities from North and South America. San Juan looked like a fairyland by night. There were cock fights and horse races, and picnics at Luquillo Beach with pigs revolving on huge spits and tables groaning with Puerto Rican delicacies.

On January 1, 1949, the whole island seemed to crowd into San Juan to watch the inaugural parade. There was an outpouring of affection toward Muñoz. He was a Puerto Rican, the first Puerto Rican elected by the people of Puerto Rico to govern them. He was the symbol of their triumph. He was the symbol of their culture and tradition, of their pride in their Spanish roots.

While I was sitting in the grandstand that day, covering the inauguration for the *New York Herald Tribune,* I saw a barefoot old man walk up to Muñoz and hand him a basket of grapefruit. The old man was a jíbaro who had walked down from the mountains to bring his gift. There was a reverent look on his face, the kind of look you sometimes see on pilgrims who come to a shrine. On this first day in the new year in the hot tropical sun of a once down-trodden island, two million people looked to Muñoz to lead them.

"With or without an oath," Muñoz said in his inaugural speech as he took the oath of office, "the forces of my conscience have fought to make my life an oath of service to my people. The great masses owe it to themselves to take this oath—that every living being better the nobility of spirit that animates it, that every hand serve better the land that it cultivates. . . . Thus the people of Puerto Rico may within the smallness of their territory realize the greatness of their destiny."

Tobacco growing on a hillside

Now the peaceful revolution was in full swing. Industries came to the island. And as Puerto Rico developed economically, as the naked were clothed and the hungry were fed, the problem of status became important again. What form of government should Puerto Rico have in its relationship with the United States? It was a two-way street. It was not only that Puerto Rico needed the United States; World War II had shown the United States how much we needed the island for its strategic location in our defense system. Great military air and naval bases were established; today the

Ramey Air Base at the northwest tip off Aguadilla is a huge self-contained city of men, planes, and equipment poised to defend the mainland or the Panama Canal.

There were three possible political roads for Puerto Rico to take vis-à-vis the United States. One was statehood. The other was independence. The third was membership in the American Union as a Commonwealth, in Spanish *Estado Libre Asociado*—Free Associated State.

Puerto Rico took the middle way. In 1952 the Commonwealth of Puerto Rico was voted into existence. It was a new political system under the American flag, so democratic and so original that it has won the admiration of most of the small nations of the world. The people of Puerto Rico write their own constitution, elect their own governor, maintain their own culture and language and traditions within the American Union. They are citizens of the United States. They are first-rate citizens of a first-rate Commonwealth in a first-rate democratic union.

This is the meaning of the Commonwealth. It is a bilateral compact signed by the people of Puerto Rico, who voted for it in a referendum, and by the Congress of the United States. Puerto Rico is no puppet government or satellite which the United States rules with tanks and commissars and secret police. It is a unique, democratic relationship in which Puerto Rico is just like a state except that it pays no federal taxes, has no voting power in Congress, and does not vote for the President.

Today there are three major political parties which represent the three roads Puerto Rico can take politically. The Popular Democratic Party is for Commonwealth. The Statehood Party is for statehood. The Independence Party is for independence.

The majority party of the land, the Popular Party, is in control not only of the Legislature but of the whole political fabric of the island. The Statehood Party, which won 26% of the votes in the 1956 elections, is the second party in power. The third group, the Independence Party, won 13% of the vote.

The program of the Popular Democratic Party is of course the program of the government—of industrializing the island, of distributing land to the landless, of educating the populace, of bridging

House of Representatives in session; Ramos Antonini,
Speaker of the House, in the Speaker's chair

the gap between the urban and the rural people. Its objective is
"a good civilization based on the abolition of poverty."

Now the question of political status has generated a new burst of
activity within the Popular Party. All over the island, young people
are being drawn into the debate. Is Commonwealth status an end
in itself; is it permanent, or is it a way station toward ultimate
statehood or independence?

"Strictly speaking, nothing in the world is permanent," Governor
Muñoz told the Puerto Rican Legislature in his 1960 Message. "I
will say that the Commonwealth status shall be as permanent as the
people of Puerto Rico may desire. . . . A government is not an
end in itself. . . . Neither is a political status. . . . The best
political status for a country is that which, with the consent of its
people, helps, or at least does not greatly hinder, the growth of its

economy and the development of what is good in its culture."

Statehood has become a burning issue on the island since Alaska, and particularly Hawaii, became states of the union. Hawaii is predominantly a multiracial land of non-Anglo-Saxons and, like Puerto Rico, is an island. Both have no contiguity to the mainland. Suddenly all over Puerto Rico posters have begun to appear, saying "51"; cars and taxicabs carry stickers on their windshields: "51." The Statehood Party has swung into action, with a simple dramatic appeal to the voters: Puerto Rico—the 51st state of the union.

The party's two leaders are Luis A. Ferré of Ponce and Miguel Angel García Méndez of Mayagüez. Ferré was born in Ponce in 1904 of an old Puerto Rican family related to Pablo Casals, studied at Massachusetts Institute of Technology, and now owns some of the largest industries of the island. In the elections for governor, held every four years, Ferré in 1956 was an unsuccessful candidate. One day in Ponce, he told me why he believed statehood was inevitable. "Federation is the most logical solution to the problem of a heterogeneous people who want to live together. Puerto Rico as a state of the union will never lose its personality. Our type of union in the United States permits Puerto Rico to retain its personality. Because it is an island it will keep its integrity. Of course we will evolve. We will contribute to the United States and they will contribute to us. We will learn English but we will never forget Spanish. Ours can be compared to the Jewish culture; it has a matrix. It has gone all over the world, but it never loses its matrix, its integrity, its character. The same with Puerto Rico. We have a matrix. We will never lose our spiritual heritage and our personality."

The Statehood Party, known also as the Statehood Republican Party, is essentially led by Puerto Rico's millionaires and draws its strength from the middle class. In Alaska, most of the millionaires I knew fought against statehood. Many of them were monopolists who had one foot on the "gravy train" and the other foot swinging free to kick everyone else off. It was the migrants with strong ties to communities they had left behind in Iowa, Minnesota, and Washington who wanted Alaska to become a state.

In Puerto Rico, many of the millionaires told me they were afraid that Commonwealth status was temporary; some day the people might vote for independence. The wealthy Puerto Ricans had investments in the United States. A few had created their own bank in Miami. They wanted to be sure that their link with the United States was permanent.

While the idea of statehood grows more popular, independence grows less popular. The leader of the Independence Party, Dr. Gilberto Concepción de Gracia, a short, stoutish man with strong Spanish features, black hair, and a mustache sprinkled with gray, is a senator-at-large in the legislature.

"They call the present regime in Spanish 'Free Associated State,'" he told me. "Yet we are not a state; neither are we free nor associated on a basis of equality with the United States. This is just colonial semantics. Independence is the only logical solution to the status question of Puerto Rico. If Puerto Rico were to become a state of the union it would become a national tragedy. Statehood is no solution for a homogeneous Latin-American community. We are a Latin-American nation. We want to govern ourselves. We want our independence."

The leaders of the Popular Democratic Party, who are today the Government of Puerto Rico, argue that statehood would mean giving up their Spanish language and culture; that independence would mean economic suicide. Statehood, they say, would mean paying taxes to the Federal treasury, and Puerto Rico could no longer attract industries to a federally tax-free island. Independence would mean choking off Puerto Rico's life ties to the United States, its freedom of trade and movement. The Populares say that without free trade with the United States, Puerto Rico would soon become a bankrupt sugar cane republic.

Although the government disagrees with the opposition parties, it actually subsidizes them to prevent the danger of a one-party government.

There is a fourth party, the Nationalists, but they have deliberately refrained since 1932 from registering at the polls. Though they are said to number about one hundred people, they are kept under close surveillance because of their acts of terrorism. Under the leadership of Pedro Albizu Campos, who is now hopelessly ill, the Nationalists have tried but failed to assassinate three governors, and a Federal judge; in 1950 they attempted to kill President Harry S. Truman. Terrorism however is completely alien to most Puerto Ricans, and even though bodyguards always surround the governor, terrorism has few advocates. This explains why the Nationalists have practically disappeared.

The island also has a handful of Communists; there are said to be fewer than fifteen Communist leaders. One of them is the novelist, César Andreu Inglesias, who spent a term in jail and wrote a book *Los Caídos*—The Fallen—about the Nationalists of Puerto Rico which won the prize of the Institute of Literature. Another, Juan Saez Corales, is now selling stationery and typewriters.

The crucial problem in Puerto Rico today is once again political. No longer a colony oppressed by Spain or neglected by the United States, the people of Puerto Rico are now struggling to find the political status that will mean more food, more jobs, and more reason for pride.

"If you follow Puerto Rican history," Gustavo Agrait, the Director of Information of the Economic Development Administration (Fomento), a thin angular man with black eyes and a small black mustache, told me one day, "you will see that ever since Spanish times, we Puerto Ricans were always middle-of-the-roaders.

"We believe colonialism ended in Puerto Rico when the compact creating the Commonwealth was signed in 1952. If we entertained any doubts, they were dispelled by Ambassador Henry Cabot Lodge when he told the United Nations that Puerto Rico now had self-government, but if the island should ever want independence, the United States would certainly grant it.

"Culturally," he said, "Puerto Rico is a Latin-American country; politically it is part of the United States. Under statehood, we would lose that culture. Moreover, Puerto Rico would be the only state in the Union which would be worse off economically the day after it became a state than it was the day before. We would immediately have to pay the Federal treasury $188,000,000 a year. Where would we get it? I believe that many of the propagandists for statehood don't really want it. Even Luis Ferré is on record in *El Mundo* and before the Congressional Committee to the effect that statehood is an economic impossibility for the time being."

In 1959 Muñoz suggested that statehood might be possible when the per capita wealth of the islanders equaled that of the poorest state of the union—Mississippi. This would happen, he thought, sometime in the 1990's.

Nearly everyone except the *Independentistas* and the *Nacionalistas* wants association with the United States; the controversy is what form that association should take. Governor Muñoz summed it up on February 23, 1960, when he welcomed Dwight D. Eisenhower at the airport in San Juan as the President began his goodwill tour of Latin America.

"You will find among us differences of opinion as to the form that our free union with the United States should develop. But, so far as the great majority of our people is concerned, you will find no difference of opinion as to the fact that that union should be permanent."

The present leaders of the government are, of course, pro-Commonwealth. In a sense, under Commonwealth, Puerto Rico has its cake and is eating it. It has all the advantages of statehood without paying federal taxes. But in a deeper sense, Commonwealth marks an evolutionary growth for an island that has come up out of colonialism into proud partnership with the fifty states of the union.

"We believe in the American Union," Dr. Arturo Morales Carrión, historian and Puerto Rico's Under Secretary of State, said. "We believe in its ideals; we know of its strength and its resilience in the spiritual field. We are not outsiders, but members of the family, however distinct we may at first glance seem to be. We have been won over, not by the kind of United States youthful nationalism, the pride of the emerging muscular giant that came to our shores in 1898, but by that deeper stream in American culture that believes in the rights of the common man, that shares its sympathy with the underdog, that is always willing to criticize itself, that constantly looks for its own shortcomings, and that, now that the United States has become a world leader, is searching with exemplary humility for a way to communicate to mankind its anguish and its compassion for the sorry trials of the human creature under the shadows of nuclear extinction."

CHAPTER 4

Muñoz and Inés

One night in Aguadilla on the northwest tip of the island, Governor Muñoz was discussing the making of a leader. "It is an agony. To be a leader is to know agony."

"But it is an honorable agony," his wife Inés said.

Muñoz nodded his head silently. He is a large brooding man, and everything about him is large—his frame, his mustache, his bushy eyebrows, his dark eyes. Even his anguish seems massive.

Yet he is not all a brooding leader sitting, like a huge marble statue, with his head in his hands. He is a Puerto Rican. He loves life, people, music, conversation, good phrases and good jokes. He is a prophetic man, with poetic insight, restless, deeply concerned with ideas and words.

He has a concrete down-to-earth humor which comes through almost everything he says. His aphorisms have become famous. "Puerto Rico," he once said, "is a land of flattering statistics and distressing realities."

To keep his people from becoming too materialistic in their search for economic prosperity, he told them: "We must live like angels and produce like the devil."

He is known affectionately as *El Vate*—the Bard. The people identify him with the island's poets, though many of the poets are

still, as he once was, for independence. "I talked to the poets in
Ponce," he told me one day. "As you know, they all want independence. I said to them, 'I am a member of a group trying to
abolish poverty. I assure you I want to abolish poverty even among
poets.' "

"A successful man," he once said, "writes poems, plants trees
and has sons. What we need in Puerto Rico are more poems and
trees."

Muñoz was born in San Juan on February 18, 1898, the son of
the Puerto Rican patriot, Luis Muñoz Rivera and Amalia Marín
de Muñoz Rivera. In the Spanish tradition he keeps his father's
name, Muñoz (pronounced Moo-NYOZ), and his mother's maiden
name Marín (pronounced Mah-REEN). He is called either Governor Muñoz or Muñoz Marín, *never* Governor Marín.

While his father served as Resident Commissioner in Washington, Muñoz was educated in the public schools of New York City
and Washington. He went to Public School 87 on Manhattan's West
Side, a school which today has an enrollment of at least 40%
Puerto Rican children. At fourteen he went to the preparatory
school of Georgetown University in Washington and took one year
of law at the University of Georgetown. But words were his interest,
not law. He moved for a short while to Greenwich Village in New
York City where he lived a bohemian life as a free-lance writer.
He translated Walt Whitman, Edwin Markham, and Carl Sandburg
into Spanish, edited a Spanish magazine, and when he was barely
nineteen, published two books *Borrones* and *Madre Haraposa*.

He married a Mississippi-born poet and great friend of Puerto
Rico, Muna Lee, in 1919 when he was 21. They had two children,
Luis Muñoz Lee, often called Luisito, and Muñita Muñoz Lee, both
of whom now live in San Juan with their children. Luisito is now
the editor of the *Island Times*. In 1926, Muñoz returned with his
family to Puerto Rico and took over his father's liberal newspaper
La Democracia. His marriage did not last and Muñoz later married
Inés María Mendoza.

Like Muñoz, Inés began her political career in favor of independence. But Muñoz was of the city and raised in the States. Inés
was of the country and raised in Puerto Rico. She was brought up

on a cattle farm on the east coast near Naguabo. Like most girls she adored her father. "I could not have known who Muñoz was, if I had not had my father," she told me one day. "My father was illiterate. He bought many books and my mother read them to him. He was a free-thinker, and my mother, who is still alive, was a devout Catholic. He valued human beings above all else. If a person would come to the house he would put aside everything and sit down and talk to that person. That was all that counted—the person to whom he was talking. He never said this to me. I was eight years old when he died but he was always taking me by the hand, talking to the workers, showing me everything on the land. The people, though, were the most important thing. He had a great deal of courage and he was very humble. I only lived with him for eight years and yet he taught me the pattern of everything good."

In the Spanish custom of Puerto Rico, Doña Inés has kept her maiden name, Mendoza, and taken on her husband's name, with a *de* before it. But formally and informally, the first lady of Puerto Rico is known simply as Doña Inés. She is a handsome, softly rounded, gracious woman with large eyes and an abundance of black hair softly framing her face. Sometimes in the evening at Jájome Alto, when she throws a dark shawl around her shoulders to ward off the cool mountain winds, she has the intensity of Pilar in Hemingway's *For Whom the Bell Tolls*. She has a passion for people, for her husband, her children born of her first marriage and of her marriage to Muñoz, and her grandchildren.

Doña Inés was a schoolteacher, teaching in elementary school, high school, and later in the Elementary Model School of the University. When she met Muñoz, she had already lost her job in the school system because she had insisted publicly that teaching all subjects in English in the Puerto Rican schools was harmful to Spanish-speaking children.

"I saw Muñoz first in one of the New Deal meetings, when he came from Washington," she described their first meeting to me. "He did not impress me very much. I thought he was one of the people in Puerto Rico who come and go. He had great influence on Roosevelt and the others in Washington. But I felt that the problem of Puerto Rico must be solved here, not in Washington. Then when

Doña Inés and young friends

he broke with the Liberal Party in 1937 and made his own program, he attracted my attention. It was when he began to teach people how to vote, that he won me over. But I never believed he would win so fast and so spectacularly in 1940.

"I knew he was a fine poet, very lonely, very honest. That impressed me. As a teacher, I always wanted to know what makes a man get people's attention immediately. Muñoz just appeared and people were attentive. He had a tremendous gift of arousing people's interest—even the people who are hostile to him. I think that is the greatest gift he has—personal magnetism. Then, too, they all know he is honest."

In the forties, Muñoz and Inés lived in a section of San Juan called Isla Verde, which was later bulldozed away to become the International Airport. Theirs was a ramshackle West Indian house with a wooden balcony where they sat while cool trade winds fanned the air, talking with people like Ed Rosskam and Jack and Irene Delano. Rosskam and Delano first came to the island in the early forties as photographers for the Farm Security Administration. But they were more than photographers. They were sociologists with cameras. They went into the hills, lived among the people, and caught on film the degradation of hunger, the beauty of the island, the undefeated spirit of the Puerto Rican people. Night after night Muñoz and Doña Inés sat with them trying to find a way. Couldn't they somehow through films or books or pamphlets get education to thousands of people who had no way of going to school?

To Muñoz the poet-politician and to Inés the teacher, illiteracy was as disastrous as hunger. They wanted not only schools for the children but schools for their parents, education for whole communities. They realized too that education was important for the growth of the new Popular Democratic Party. These were the people who made up the party. The people had great native peasant wisdom, but Muñoz knew that his party would not mature and grow unless his followers had a better knowledge of what was going on in the world.

They had been oppressed. They had been governed foolishly or wickedly. They had been hungry. Their babies had died of malnutrition and dysentery. But the strength that had kept them alive through the centuries of grinding poverty was the strength that Muñoz was now trying to draw out of them.

He won through. Today he controls his party completely. Perhaps too completely. For one looks over the island for the young leaders who must some day take over. This was a revolution of young men and young women who in 1940 were in their thirties and early forties. Now they are middle-aged and older. They face the same dilemma that one sees in India, where a truly great leader seems to draw all the political strength of the land into himself. A few people have suggested that a likely successor might be Roberto Sánchez Vilella who is Secretary of State and who has been close to Muñoz for twenty-five years. Others have suggested Fernando Sierra Berdecía, the Secretary of Labor.

One day I asked Sánchez Vilella, "How does it feel to work in the shadow of a man like Muñoz?"

He leaned forward across his desk. "Muñoz is a great man to work for. He's demanding, exacting, driving. He demands an

Sentry box, part of San Juan's old fortifications, looking toward La Fortaliza

answer to his challenge, an intellectual and physical answer. He gives no quarter. He works as hard as any of us. But he is so stimulating and so warm, and so thoroughly honest and whole, that it's exciting to work with him. I never worked for anyone else for whom I had so much respect. Even if he's convinced you're wrong, if he believes you are honest, he'll listen to you and never become impatient. He'll let you argue six months. He only gets impatient if he feels that somehow you are trying to put something over on him. If he feels that you have no ulterior motives, there is no problem. The prerequisite is that you come with clean hands."

I have met Europeans who, thinking of Puerto Rico in the framework of Latin-American dictatorships, have asked if Puerto Rico had a strong military force to back up the man in power. Did it have generals? Did the generals want to take over the government? Did the governor stay in power with the connivance and support of the hundred-odd rich families? Were there military plots? Was this government-in-a-revolving door, with each man assassinating the man who preceded him?

It astonished them to find that the revolution in Puerto Rico was a bloodless revolution at the polls. The military played no role at all. The only military in Puerto Rico are the United States Armed Forces and the Puerto Rican National Guard. These are a relaxed people and, though politics is in the air they breathe, they are not a violent people.

To be sure Muñoz has passionate political enemies. The State-hood leaders call him authoritarian, overpaternalistic, too acquies-cent to labor; some call him a dictator. The *Independentistas* say he has betrayed his early ideals of independence. But even his most vociferous opponents tell you he is incorruptible. Carlos J. Torres, a silver-haired aristocrat, a former bank director, and, like most of the very wealthy, a member of the Statehood Republican Party, told me one day, "Anybody who knows the Puerto Rican people and their history knows that they don't vote for an idea. They vote for a man. For three hundred years they have voted for a man. Whatever Muñoz wants, they want. But Muñoz is an outstanding man. Very honest."

Muñoz is known to be a poor man. The only thing he owns is his modest house at Trujillo Alto, half an hour's drive from San Juan. La Fortaleza and the summer house in the mountains at Jájome Alto belong to the government. When salary raises were passed in the Legislature a few years ago, he refused to accept an increase. The next governor will receive the increase.

In the late thirties, one of the founders of the Popular Demo-cratic Party lent Muñoz his car, but there was always the problem of finding money to buy gasoline. One morning Muñoz discovered he and Inés had 26 cents. They had a choice of buying breakfast or buying gasoline to drive to a political meeting in another town. They drove.

Muñoz' day begins about six or seven in the morning. He has a large wood-paneled office in the 400-year-old palace at La Fortaleza. Actually his office is wherever his papers are. And his papers are everywhere, in his bedroom, in the library next to the bedroom. Anybody else would be lost looking at the papers stacked in the library, but Muñoz knows exactly where everything is. "Oh, yes," he will tell you, "you want that clipping we were talking about last week. I have it in the library. It's next to a red ruler with a yellow clip on it."

Muñoz is an off and on sleeper. He may wake up at one in the morning, start reading, doze off at four, and be up at six for the whole day. He may start reading some report, have breakfast in his room, and perhaps at eight in the morning have a secretary come upstairs to take notes. He spends his morning reading and dictating.

At twelve sharp though he has lunch. It is a family affair at La Fortaleza with Doña Inés and their two daughters, Victoria, whom they call Melo, 19, Viviana, 20, and Viviana's husband and baby, Victoria Inés.

After lunch, he goes back to the bedroom, takes something to read, and naps. About one-thirty or two he goes downstairs to his official office. The difference between his office downstairs and the library upstairs is a subtle one. The papers are stacked the same way; there are piles of books to be read, magazines to be looked at. The whole world interests him, though Puerto Rico is his life. He schedules fifteen-minute interviews with his staff, cabinet members, government officials, and important visitors.

Inés, who presides completely over their home, helped Muñoz settle down and get some routine into his life. "Twenty years ago," Sánchez Vilella told me, "Muñoz was the sort of fellow who would start a conversation at two o'clock in the afternoon and wind up at two the next afternoon. We might be sitting in the Legislature when it was in session and at the end of a tough day he would decide we should go to El Yunque (the rain forest), stay overnight, and come back to the Legislature the next morning at eight. He was really a fellow to follow around. Now he is still capable of working twenty-four hours but at least he's home for a while."

There are people who say Inés has too much influence. There are those who talk of the Doña Inés type of thinking—symbolized by a

El Yunque, the rain forest

love of the Spanish culture and tradition. There are some who say
that she sometimes pulls the Governor too far back toward those
traditions and to Spain, while others are pulling him forward toward
greater industrialization and Americanization. But there are also
those who say this is a good thing—Puerto Rico's strength lies in

her Spanish *and* American traditions. Puerto Rico is the bridge between the United States and the Caribbean, between the United States and South America.

Doña Inés is Muñoz' conscience. She never lets him forget his basic aims—the aims that brought him his first victories in 1940. She guards him, protects him from growing too tired, travels with him constantly on the island or back and forth to the States.

"I see him when he goes to bed every night," she once told me. "He falls asleep slowly, always thinking. When he wakes up he is thinking—always about Puerto Rico. Always of the island and the people."

Late one afternoon we were sitting in the lovely gardens of La Fortaleza. Doña Inés was dressed in white, her only jewelry a large gold wedding ring and a choker of white pearls.

"You know that phrase the bullfighters use: 'the moment of truth?' " I said. "What do you think is Puerto Rico's moment of truth?"

She leaned back in her chair and looked up at the tall majestic Royal Palms. It was the beginning of the quiet hour. *Reinitas,* tiny black and yellow birds called "little queens," were flittering through the palms.

"I would say the people," she replied. "The people have extraordinary quality. To do what they have done after so many centuries of neglect both from Spain and from the United States. Not to deteriorate. As my husband says, 'being gallant enough not to accept despair.' When you go to the country, you can still see the qualities that make these people. You can see how they have changed this island. You cannot say that it is Muñoz. You cannot say that it is the party or Fomento or 'Bootstrap.' It is the people."

CHAPTER 5

Industrialization Is the Hope of the Poor

Fomento is the backbone of the revolution in Puerto Rico.

Along the highways from San Juan to Mayagüez the new trademark of the island is a billboard showing a strong-muscled laborer pushing the wheel of industry. Behind the billboard is a new factory, one of the 600 factories which Fomento has encouraged in the last fifteen years. In English Fomento is EDA—the Economic Development Administration. But all over Puerto Rico, the *Administración de Fomento Económico* is called simply Fomento.

This is a proud land and Fomento is the pride of Puerto Rico. For Fomento is more than industries. It is Puerto Rico's new way of life.

Fomento is a kind of cradle-to-grave welfare program for industry. No country in the world has worked out so imaginative a program of inducing industry, from the mainland or abroad, to expand its operations away from home. Other countries are far more advanced technologically. But it is in the technique of promotion that Puerto Rico is unique.

Here is a country which tells business it is wanted, tells capital it is not a big bad wolf, and yet is wholly sympathetic to labor.

Indian and Arab visitors at the Puerto Nuevo
Steam Power Plant in San Juan

The touchstone to the men running Fomento is that they are not doctrinaire. They play by ear. Though most of them grew up in Puerto Rico as liberals, pro-labor, they learned quickly that they could love capital more and still not love labor less. The more investment capital that came in, the more industries that were started, the more jobs that were created, the more labor itself was benefited and the island lifted out of poverty.

How did Fomento get started? I asked this of Mariano Ramírez,

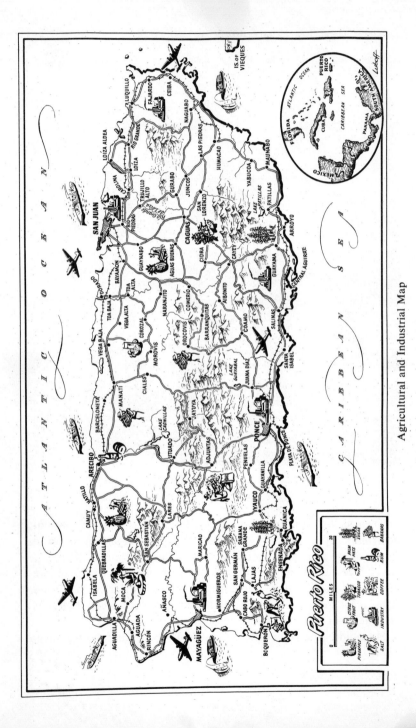

Agricultural and Industrial Map

the general counsel for Fomento, one day at lunch in the Swiss Chalet in San Juan. He was one of the original planners.

"Fomento really began in 1942," he said, "soon after the Popular Democratic Party came to power. Tugwell, who was governor at the time, had already picked Ted Moscoso as a brilliant assistant. Moscoso immediately began to look for ways of improving industry on the island.

"We had laws then that gave tax exemption. But they worked against us. They protected the infant industries that we had and they kept other industries out. Moscoso asked stateside economists to make a study. They all pointed out what industries we Puerto Ricans could create ourselves. But nobody thought of attracting industries from the mainland or abroad."

Ramírez, one of the island's successful lawyers, could have passed as a "perfect" Aryan, with blond hair, a blond mustache, and fair skin. He continued the background story of Fomento in flawless English.

"Rum had become an important industry because Scotch wasn't available when the war began in December 1941. Rum is especially important here. In the liquor industry the Government is the big partner because of high taxes. We were exporting a lot of rum to the States. But the rum industry was handicapped by a lack of glass bottles. We tried to get Owens Glass and other big firms to build a bottle plant. They all begged off because of war work. So we went to Washington, got priorities, and began to build our own glass bottle plant—one of the most complicated and difficult plants to operate. Then we found that we had bottles but no cartons in which to ship the bottles. So our second plant was a paper plant for cartons.

"When the war ended and the restrictions were lifted, Moscoso changed the whole program. It was difficult for government to be in management and deal with labor. Moscoso decided that the Puerto Rican Government would no longer own and manage industries. We would sell the plants we had built, and use government funds for seed money, to induce industry to come down. And we would set up a sales organization to sell the Fomento idea. It would be a catalyst for private enterprise. The government sold the glass and

paper plant to the Ferré interests and now set about selling manufacturers in the States the idea of opening plants in Puerto Rico."

Tax exemption became the greatest inducement. "We went to
Muñoz in 1946," Ramírez said, "with the idea of offering industry
some tax exemption. Muñoz was the one who made it a tax holiday."

Industry began to come down to the island. The first plant was
the Red Cape Leather Company in the little town of Cabo Rojo
next to Mayagüez. It was a branch of the "House of Nash" in Jersey
City, and today its owner is a millionaire.

In its present form, the program really gained momentum by
1949. By 1960 nearly 600 factories were at work on the island.

All over Puerto Rico, buildings are now waiting in nearly every
one of the seventy-six towns for Fomento's salesmen to find manufacturers to fill them. They are finding them all over the United
States, and all over the world. Four or five factories have come
from Europe, one making rubber fittings, another making life-like
plastic flowers. All are shipping their products to the States. A
factory from Spain is making plastic flowers; a Canadian plant is
making screws and bolts; a Hawaiian company is making candy
and extracting oil syrup out of Puerto Rico's coconuts.

The firms that have come to Puerto Rico have invested over half
a billion dollars on the island. Branches of some of the largest firms
in the United States are writing new success stories on the island—
Remington Rand, General Electric, Consolidated Cigar, Beaunit
Mills, International Shoe, Proctor Electric, American Can, Phelps
Dodge, Firth Carpet, Van Raalte Gloves, the Carborundum Company, Sperry Rand, W. R. Grace and Company, Parke, Davis and
Company, Sunbeam Corporation, Molinos de Puerto Rico (a
branch of Nebraska Consolidated Mills of Omaha), Union Carbide
Corporation, Standard Brands, Savage Arms, and the Borden Com-
pany among others.

These industries come for many reasons. There is no political
risk for an American investor in Puerto Rico; there is no fear of
sudden restrictions or expropriation; there is no danger of revolution and of panic flight. The American dollar is as good in San Juan
as it is in Wall Street. Through Puerto Rico, investors have a logical

Puerto Rico Cement Corporation at Cataño

jumping-off place to the markets of both North and South America. With the American flag on the island, there is economic as well as political security, with freedom of movement for employers, employees, the products they make and the money they earn. The island has free access to the richest market in the world.

There are other reasons, too. Puerto Rico has cheaper labor than the mainland and good climate. And most important of all, it has tax exemption.

The *Wall Street Journal* called Puerto Rico a "taxpayers' paradise." Certainly Puerto Rico offers industries tax incentives offered by few other countries in the world. It exempts the employer from paying income tax to the Commonwealth Government for ten years.

Thus an industry opening a new branch on the island is assured of paying no income tax to the Commonwealth for ten years and no tax to the Federal Government.

"For all practical purposes, industries coming here pay no taxes at all," Hubert C. Barton, a white-haired New Deal economist who is now Fomento's director of the Office of Economic Research, told me. "A company which expands fast enough can actually avoid taxes, because at the end of the ten years they start on 'flexible depreciation.' Without that depreciation they do pay local taxes. But even then local corporate taxes are 21% to 37% as compared with 52% in the United States."

A survey by Fomento published in March 1960 showed that three quarters of the firms whose ten-year Commonwealth tax exemption would soon expire, stated that they planned to remain on the island. Many firms may have come for the tax holiday, but now, even without tax exemption, they wanted to stay.

Fomento has offices in New York City, Chicago, Miami, and Los Angeles, with well-equipped staffs to give manufacturers a complete picture of the island's possibilities. It is almost a government within a government, with some thirty-eight separate divisions which include everything from the Department of Tourism, a hotel school, and rum promotion to gambling supervision.

The head of Fomento is Teodoro Moscoso. A tireless, hard-working executive, Moscoso is both a doer and a thinker. In any land he could be a top business or government executive. Here he is one of the country's top executives, a leader without political ambition. It is enough to be the economic catalyst of an island in ferment. It is enough to know that each day, with each new contract Fomento signs, he is providing employment for more Puerto Ricans. He started out in Ponce in his father's business, now one of a chain of successful drug stores which his family still runs. Like most of the executives in this island government, he came into his job with high ideals and little experience. As the job grew, he grew.

He is a man of impatient vision. He may give one of his top men an assignment that should take two weeks; the next morning he is sure to call on the phone, "Have you got it done?" He never seems to look back, or to waste time in recriminations. His soul-searching

The Caribe-Hilton Hotel, on the ocean; two-story building
in foreground is the Supreme Court Building

is focused on the future. He never loses sight of his goal, fortifying
both industry and agriculture. His dream is an industrial standard
of living for his people with moral and social values.

His office, in a ten-story building at Stop 22, is as functional and
uncluttered as his thinking. One morning we were discussing the
Puerto Rican revolution, when his phone rang. New York was on
the line. An oil executive was flying down for a quick talk with the
economic boss of the island. On the phone Moscoso talked like the
economic boss. As soon as he hung up, he returned to the philosophy of the revolution. He handed me a British journal he had been
reading the night before. "Look at these words by Sir Charles P.
Snow," he said. " 'Industrialization is the only hope of the poor.'

"This is what I believe. Our people are getting three meals a day.

Fomento is a way of employing people so that they will stay in Puerto Rico. But for those who want to emigrate to the States, Fomento does the second-best job by preparing them for migration. They go knowing about the time clock. The time clock means many things. It means taking the train on time, learning to measure things. These are things you don't learn in a primitive agricultural economy.

"The important thing, perhaps the most important thing, in Fomento is that we are trying not to lose our souls. We're trying not to be only materialists; we have to worry about our minds and spirits, too. We don't want to distort our personality in a rush for industry. Surely there will be some losses, but the gains will counteract them.

"We had to think of incentives. Take tourism. It was a vicious cycle. Tourists wouldn't come because there were no facilities. There were no facilities because there were no tourists. So Fomento started the Caribe-Hilton Hotel. We built the hotel and leased it to Mr. Hilton to operate. Its success taught us that tourism is one of the industries we could best promote."

"What industries are you specially eager to attract now?" I asked him.

"Particularly those," he said, "that require high skills. We shall have to specialize like the Swiss. It will take generations but we will have to start now teaching fathers and sons. Since we have no raw materials, we'll have to go into industries that require the dexterity our people have—like machining of metals, or the making of delicate and small instruments like watches and clocks. Already we are in the polishing of diamonds. Every day diamonds go to the States in little match boxes. We need something intricate that can be passed on from father to son. We will lose some of it through migration to New York and the States, but with better wages our people will stay here. Weston and General Electric are already making light meters. This is as close to watch-making as you can get. We have a watch factory—Timex. One of the things we like about the metal industries is that they normally use men. One of our big problems is that most of the new industries coming in are light industries using women."

Others told me the island could use more supermarkets, restaurants, small hotels, motels, intensive truck gardeners, contractors to build private homes, and almost any industry allied with tourism. Puerto Rico has few raw materials but it has climate and beauty. And it has people. People are its greatest natural resource.

The fiscal year which ended June 30, 1959, was the island's best year to date in industrial production. Some 41,000 people were working in Fomento plants as compared with 33,000 people the year before. One hundred thirty-six stateside firms signed contracts with Fomento in 1959 compared with 91 in 1958. Fifty-three local firms whose control is in the hands of Puerto Ricans were opened or expanded in 1959 as compared with 47 the year before. Average Fomento wages, which were 86 cents an hour in 1958, went up to 90 cents an hour in 1959.

Before a man comes to Puerto Rico to sign a contract, much of the research has already been done for him. If his problem is a technical one, he will be taken to Moe Moses, also an ex-Washington hand. Moses believes in the "soft sell." He tells the industrialist all the disadvantages as well as the advantages of coming to the island, the problems of marketing, of transportation, of training managers as well as labor. Some manufacturers are discouraged; others sign a contract with PRIDCO, the Puerto Rico Industrial Development Company, twenty-four hours after they arrive.

"The greatest inducement," Moses told me, "is that most firms complete paying all their costs in less than five years. Many people are shocked when they hear of the high profits made in Puerto Rico. Most firms make at least 16 to 20% profit here; others more. But we are realists. We feel there is no moral issue. We recognize that a man has many problems here, transportation, working in a strange culture, etc. We know he will come only if he can make a big profit."

In most economies, making "a big profit" might mean gouging the profit out of the backs of the people. But Fomento points out that in Puerto Rico this profit means putting food into mouths that were hungry. It means giving decent wages to people who had slave wages or no wages at all. It means starting channels of trade; it means more money in the treasury to add more rural and urban schools to the 10,939 schoolrooms now on the island, to increase the 4,624 miles of highways that encircle the country, to bring the hills closer to San Juan and the industries into the hinterland.

The new industries have helped raise the annual earnings from $125 per capita in 1940 to $514 in 1960, second only to Venezuela in Latin America. The sugar cane industry, still the largest employer on the island, employs 65,000 people, but they work only during the five-month sugar harvest. Most of the 41,000 in the new industries are employed all year.

Nor are workers in the States thrown out of jobs by industries that might be tempted to move their entire operations to Puerto Rico because of the tax holiday. Fomento will sign no contract with a firm that shuts down in the States; it will only sign with a firm that expands or builds a subsidiary on the island.

Working on a grass-roots level, Fomento has set up ten "Industrial Promotion Committees" in towns throughout the island. These committees are made up of a cross section of the leading industrialists, bankers, merchants, lawyers, educators, civic and religious leaders. Each town appoints its own members who usually meet for lunch once a week. Fomento has a representative in most of the communities, and a field man who travels around the island helping the committees co-ordinate their activities. It is industry's self-help program.

The industrial committees which I met in Ponce, San Germán, and Mayagüez were made up of forceful community leaders, all working to induce industries to come to their towns. Some of the men were politically in the "loyal opposition," in favor of statehood or independence, but they were all completely pro-Fomento. There was good-humored but genuine rivalry among the towns outbidding each other in offering new inducements to be added to Fomento's tax exemptions.

Fomento has learned from hard experience that some housewives who come to the island with their manager husbands may need help. A whole enterprise may be destroyed by an unhappy wife, unable to adjust to a new culture.

Under Dr. Leo Suslow, the young Director of Industrial Services and a native New Yorker, Fomento helps the housewife find a home, helps find schools for her children, shows her where to shop, helps her get a telephone, sets up women's clubs, and tries to find good household help.

The Fomento picture is not all bright. While there are 600 new plants now in operation, some 200 other plants have closed down, a failure rate which compares quite favorably with the rate in the United States. Some industries have left the island entirely; others have stayed but have cut their plants down to small operations. The major reasons for closing have been the drying up of markets in the United States, poor management, and insufficient initial financing. Some have attributed their closing to rising wages and labor problems. Others have complained that Fomento has not given them all the help that was promised. Still others complain that even though Fomento, a branch of the government, is pro-management, the government itself is more likely to side with labor in a crucial dispute. With most plants on the island, the first two or three years tell the story. If they can last two years, they can usually remain in business.

One of the criticisms of Fomento is that some of its representatives in the States oversell the advantages of Puerto Rico, promise "pie in the sky" and then don't deliver. A frantic New York manufacturer collared me in the Fomento building one day, crying, "What this country is doing to my ulcer! What bureaucrats! I got a taxi waiting downstairs. I gotta be at the airport to catch a plane in twenty minutes. Make them put everything in writing or they'll eat your heart out."

"Are you going through with your project?" I asked him.

"Sure," he said, and caught his taxi.

The manager of a successful firm from New England told me one day, "We're down here and we're going to stay down here. We're doing o.k.; if we weren't, we'd fold up and go back to the mainland. But it's not all roses. I'd say that absenteeism is our biggest problem. We aren't getting the full benefit of a trained worker because we hire mostly women. They're always having babies. We have to pay them for eight-weeks' maternity leave. At the same time we have to hire and train someone else during that time who works with only about 50% effectiveness."

He had touched the core of Puerto Rico's crucial problem of

overpopulation. Every facet of life on the island is affected by the "population explosion." Fomento too is learning what India and Indonesia and other underdeveloped countries have discovered to their sorrow, that industrialization cannot succeed in a runaway population. Before Fomento can create 20,000 new jobs, there are 40 to 60,000 new teen-agers and adults ready to join the labor force.

Many manufacturers complain that they train their workers in Puerto Rico only to lose them in the migration pull to the States. "Puerto Rico is a training ground for skills in Chicago, Philadelphia, Rochester, and New York," a stateside manager in San Juan told me. "It's very good for the employers in the States but it's hard for Puerto Rico. Our companies spend the money to train them and we lose them to companies in the States who offer them higher wages."

Before Fomento was created, the major industry on the island was sugar, and rum was the child of sugar. Rum is as much a part of Puerto Rico as its palm trees and its cool trade winds. Actually the story of rum goes back eight hundred years before the Christian era when an unsung farmer in the hinterland of Asia ground his sugar cane into molasses and drank it. Columbus brought sugar to the New World on his second voyage and Ponce de León brought it to the island from Hispaniola. Today Puerto Rico is the world's greatest producer of rum. Nearly 75% of the rums sold in the United States are distilled in Puerto Rico. About $20,000,000 a year in taxes on rum shipped to the mainland fill the coffers of the Commonwealth treasury.

Local wits say that rum is the real "spirit" behind Operation Bootstrap. Others, mixing their metaphors but not their drinks, insist that Fomento is "floated" by rum. Certainly much of the Fomento program is financed by the $10.50 a proof gallon in excise taxes which Puerto Rico's rum distillers pay to the Federal Government, which in turn gives it to the Puerto Rican treasury.

The boom in rum began in 1941 at the beginning of World War II. From 1945 to 1948, the distilleries of Puerto Rico worked day and night, and Sundays and holidays, squeezing the essence of the sugar cane into 16,679,000-proof gallons of Puerto Rican rum.

But in the rush to fill the demand, much of the rum shipped north was unaged, inferior, and even unpalatable. As soon as other alcohols were available, the market for rum dropped disastrously. In 1948, barely 317,000-proof gallons were sold in the States. In Puerto Rico itself rum continued to be the national drink.

But now Fomento was in existence. The government decided to retrieve the good name the Puerto Rican rum had had before the "boom and bust" period. It realized that the rum industry, healthy again, could help launch Operation Bootstrap. The government passed the Commonwealth Mature Spirits Act requiring that all Puerto Rican rums were to be properly aged and blended. It set up the "Puerto Rico Rum Pilot Plant" on the grounds of the University of Puerto Rico, a seven-story white concrete laboratory with instruments to test every single stage of rum distilling. The government's work has paid off. In 1959 Fomento, though it puts no money into the industry, spent $1,150,000 to promote the rums of Puerto Rico. The tax income from rum in 1957 was $18,000,000. Two years later it was touching $20,000,000, a record level.

The Big Three, the island's largest distillers, are the Puerto Rican Distilling Company in Arecibo, some sixty miles from San Juan, where Ronrico and Rum Llave are produced; Bacardi, which was started in Cuba, has had a branch in Puerto Rico for twenty-one years, and now has opened one of the world's largest distilleries in San Juan; and the Destilería Seralles at Ponce, which produces the famous Don Q and Boca Chica. There are actually sixteen rum producers in Puerto Rico; eight of them are distillers and eight buy their distillates from the first eight, then age, color, and blend the rum in their own secret formula and bottle it.

But rum is no solution to the island's labor problem. The entire industry employs barely 1,000 workers a year. And even the profits of the Big Three, after taxes, are all held in tightly closed family corporations. The Seralles family in Ponce was the richest family on the island until the last decade when they were surpassed by the Ferrés of Ponce. The reception room of their Don Q plant in Ponce is a blue-and-white bar where visitors are fed rum and cigarettes by Tito Wirshing, a member of the Board, whose father, a German from Bremen, married one of the Seralles girls. Tito, with a blond, graying beard and mustache, is not only the official greeter, but the "Governor" of the famous little island off Ponce called "Dead Men's Chest."

Tourism has been one of Fomento's most spectacular successes. It started when Fomento opened the Caribe-Hilton Hotel in December 1949. At first the scheme seemed so harebrained and doomed to failure that it was called "Moscoso's Folly." The whole burden of the hotel seemed to be Puerto Rico's. Mr. Hilton's only risk was $300,000 which he invested in silver, china, uniforms, food, etc. Fomento's initial investment was $7,200,000. The folly turned into the success story of the decade. Hilton made 100% profit every year, tax free, and Fomento has already gotten back all of its investment. Hilton pays Fomento two thirds of everything he makes in the hotel and gambling casino. Tourists sitting around the green baize tables playing roulette or 21 and losing heavily, have the rueful satisfaction of knowing that they are leaving a good part of their money to the Government of Puerto Rico.

What Fomento did in building the Caribe-Hilton Hotel and leasing it was then copied by other countries who built hotels and invited Hilton to run them. Now other hotel chains are following the same pattern. The Sheraton chain has already bought a large plot of land in San Juan for a four-hundred-room oceanside hotel. Since the opening of the Hilton, Fomento has built La Concha Hotel in San Juan and has invested money in the San Juan Intercontinental Hotel, La Rada Hotel in San Juan, the Dorado Beach Hotel in Dorado, and the Ponce Intercontinental Hotel. It has also invested money in expanding and improving many of the smaller hotels, such as the Hotel Villa Parguera in La Parguera, a charming fisherman's village on the southwestern coast, El Rosario in a California-like mountain setting between San Germán and Mayagüez, the Barranquitas Hotel in Barranquitas at the center of the island, and the Montemar on the northwestern coast in Aguadilla.

Now the tourist industry is booming. In 1958, 220,000 tourists came and spent $35,000,000. In 1959, 260,000 came and spent $42,000,000. Overnight the island has become a year-round resort as tourists have discovered that the summers are barely five degrees warmer than the winters, with cooling trade winds, and that gen-

The New Ponce Intercontinental Hotel

erally the only two hot months are September and October when the trade winds usually die.

To keep the flavor of Puerto Rico, to prevent it from becoming another Miami Beach with only hotels along the ocean shore, Fomento's Tourist Division has set up regulations limiting the number of hotels in the Candado section of San Juan. Hotel builders are induced to find attractive tourist spots around the island. And, to prevent Puerto Rico from becoming another Las Vegas, Fomento regulates casinos. It has divided the island into three sections for the purpose of regulating gambling casinos. The minimum investment in a new hotel to warrant a gambling casino license in San Juan is $5,000,000. In the second section of the island it is $2,000,000, and in the third section it is $1,000,000.

Tourists bring money with them, spreading it indirectly around the island. But it is the new Fomento factories, with their regular

Friday afternoon payroll, which reach directly into the homes of every one of their workers. Slowly their houses change from a little shack to a concrete home. Soon the house has a television antenna on its roof and a big white refrigerator in the living room. After a while there is a car in front of the house. In the nearby town the stores are stocked with clothes and furniture; the store fronts are freshly painted; the music pouring out of the restaurants and bars and dry-goods stores sounds gayer than ever.

It was James T. Whittenton, the president and manager of Caribe General Electric, Inc. in Palmer (pronounced PALM-AIR), a soft-voiced man with kindly blue eyes peering through his glasses, who decided to pay one-week's salary to his 530 employees in silver dollars. He wanted to do two things. He wanted to show the employees themselves how much money they were taking home each week, and he wanted to show the merchants how much of the G.E. payroll finds its way into their cash registers. It turned out to be an economic object lesson—demonstrating what an industry could do for a community.

Two armored trucks brought $16,000 in silver dollars to the plant: the rest of the payroll was in five-dollar and ten-dollar bills. The silver dollars were put in little white pouches like the gold-dust pouches that miners used in Alaska.

"We paid our employees on Friday afternoon," Mr. Whittenton told me. "The next Tuesday at 3 P.M. we sent a representative from our personnel office into the community to see where the money went. He visited 104 different stores and shops within a radius of fifteen miles of the factory. Out of the $16,000 paid in silver dollars, we accounted for all but $1,000 that probably never got into circulation. Many kept a few silver dollars as keepsakes and gifts. We established that $3,000 got into Santurce, a section of San Juan, as payments on white goods—refrigerators, washing machines, stoves, TV sets, radios, mixers, toasters, mostly for Mother's Day gifts.

"We found $5,800 in our little Barrio of Palmer that very Tuesday. $5,300 of that money turned up in the cash boxes of five general stores. They sell roofing, windows, beer, paint, foodstuffs and many other household items. Everyone in our community got stirred up about those silver dollars. We even found thirty silver dollars in a little bar restaurant in the hills. One fellow worked his regular work week with considerable overtime including Sunday (double time) and that week his pay envelope contained $194. We couldn't get all the silver dollars in one canvas bag or even two so had to pay him partly in paper money."

Mr. Whittenton took us on a tour of the plant. Both men and women were making residential and small industrial-type circuit breakers on conveyor belts. "Think of people who never worked in industry before being able to make such a complicated circuit breaker.

"Unlike many of the other industries on the island which employ only women, Caribe General Electric employs twice as many men as women. The plant works a three-shift day, which starts at 6:30 in the morning. Women are not allowed to work on the late shifts, since in Puerto Rico, by law, women cannot work in a factory after 10 P.M. and our second shift is over at 11:30 P.M."

As we walked around the plant, we heard men singing Spanish and English songs. We saw women dressed in white and pastel dresses, starched and crisp, looking up from their intricate work to smile at us. I talked with a man who had worked in New York as a toolmaker in Long Island City and had just returned to the island to work in this factory's tool room. His name was Ralph Meléndez; he was 32 years old. "I went to New York thirteen years ago," he said. "I went to school and then joined the U. S. Army."

"Why did you leave New York to return home?" I asked him.

"New York is no good for children," he said. "No good to raise them there. I am happy to be back home with my family."

Though some Fomento plants may go back to the States after their ten-year period of tax exemption runs out, everyone is sure that Caribe General Electric is in Puerto Rico to stay. There are now four G.E. affiliate plants in the island employing a total of over 1,000 people.

Mr. Whittenton has turned the plant into more than an important industry in a federally tax-exempt island. He has turned it into a community project with a social awareness that is being studied and, where possible, copied by other industries.

"We put out a little newspaper every Friday," he told me. "It's our *Herald Tribune* and the *Wall Street Journal* of the hills wrapped up in one. The people won't go home on Friday unless they have two things—their pay and their paper. The newspaper tells all about the plant and the activities in the lives of our employees and I write a half-page column every week to keep the employees informed as to items of interest and importance to them. We have about sixty leaders in the community—priests, ministers, the general store manager, the postmaster, the filling station man, etc. They, too, get a copy of our newspaper. In this way they will know first-hand what we are doing. We want them to feel that we are a good industrial force in the community and that we want to help them to make this a better community. If someone should say, 'Hey, have you heard about the big speed-up program in that sweatshop in Palmer' or some other derogatory remark, our readers in the community, who read our paper, can correct any misstatements and tell them the truth.

"Our employees are very loyal. They will work very well. However, we have had to teach them many things about industrial hygiene and work habits. Our toilet facilities are better than in many of their homes.

"We built rest rooms for them to use. We take them home in the station wagon when they become ill since most of them live up in the hills. People often play up how emotional the Puerto Ricans are, how easy it is to hurt their feelings, but if you can find a way to show them that you are interested in their welfare, your major problem is overcome.

"Before I came to Puerto Rico many people told me that the Puerto Ricans were slow to learn and while they did have good manual dexterity they were not fitted to do our type of work. Time has proved those people to be wrong since our Puerto Rican workers are producing our complex devices with excellent quality and productivity."

Outside of Caguas, eighteen miles from San Juan, is a long pink stucco building inlaid with colorful tiles. In front of the building is a Fomento sign—Consolidated Cigar Corporation of Puerto Rico. It is wholly owned by the largest cigar company in the world and is the largest employer on the island. In Caguas alone 1,400 workers handle tobacco and turn out cigars; another thousand will work in the new 540,000-square-foot plant being built by the company in Cayey, twelve miles from Caguas.

Francisco Verdiales, the fifty-two-year-old Puerto Rican-born manager of Consolidated Cigar is a prototype of the new Puerto Rican executive. He had been a high Labor Department official and also a Fomento executive. It was he who created the Industrial Services Department of Fomento to look after the interests of the new firms establishing factories on the island. Consolidated Cigar hired him from Fomento to become their personnel manager. Soon they recognized his abilities and made him vice-president and general manager.

Thin, smiling, with tortoise-shell glasses and an easy-going manner with his employees, most of whom he calls by their first names, he looks like a college professor on a campus. Yet he is considered one of the outstanding executives on the island, with a deep concern for the problems of his people and an intellectual approach to the problem of management and labor. He works in the plant all day and at night teaches at the University of Puerto Rico, giving such courses as Wage and Salary Administration, Industrial Relations, History of the Labor Movement, and Labor Legislation.

Walking through the factory with its partitioned doors, we suddenly came upon the wonderful smell of pure tobacco. The air seemed filled with sweet molasses. Pretty girls in bright earrings, wearing green or gray uniforms over their dresses, stood in long lines feeding the conveyor belt machines, making cigars, packaging cigars, and boxing them. "Our workers here can make as many cigars as the machines allow them to make," Verdiales said. "Our workers are as good as you'll find anywhere in the world, if properly screened and trained. We used to check for hand dexterity before we hired them. But it's not necessary. They have it. Born, I guess. All these psychological gadgets, we don't need them with this type of person. The good workers of Puerto Rico and the good managerial know-how of the mainland have made this operation a success.

"Mostly women work here. It's a tradition in this industry even in the States. Women have worked cigar machines ever since they were invented. While the women are here, the men work in agriculture. But that's seasonal work. So, many women are earning much more than their men. Our industry is changing the lives of the women in the hills and in the five or six neighboring towns from which they come. The Spanish woman is becoming more independent. Men will have to take it. Now family life has a new slant. Woman stands on a pedestal in her home. She brings in money; she has a new importance. Gradually women are becoming more important in the community too.

"Our salaries are above average in Puerto Rico. When we began training workers for this plant in 1952, the legal minimum wage was 35 cents an hour. Voluntarily we made it 40 cents an hour. Through the years we went along with constructive increases until today, when the legal minimum is 85 cents, our average is about one dollar an hour. Of course, the Puerto Rican wage levels are constantly improving as the economy of the island permits. In the States the legal minimum is $1.00 for our work, but they pay more I understand. The differential in total costs between the States and Puerto Rico must be there, otherwise it wouldn't pay them to come way down here to set up a factory."

We were sitting now in his office while we talked. Outside his window the lawn was green and beautifully trimmed. The whole plant looked like a country club.

It was lunchtime and crowds of girls dressed in attractive cotton dresses and high-heeled shoes walked under umbrellas down the hot sun-splattered road to their homes. Some of the women jumped into cars to drive home. Others ate their lunch on the green lawn, under beautiful *flamboyan* trees, or in the huge sunny and air-conditioned dining room of the plant cafeteria where 350 people could sit down at one time to a solid Spanish lunch for about fifty cents a meal. At one end of the dining room there was a huge, brilliantly colored mural, painted in 1956 by a talented artist who signs himself simply Arana. It showed the life and customs of the island, with men playing cards, couples dancing, musicians strumming guitars, a cockfight, a blindfold game, and a man in a procession carrying a painting of the Three Kings.

"This plant has the highest payroll on the island," Mr. Verdiales said. "Over $40,000 per week, every week of the year. Nobody employs more people under one roof than we do, and we are proud of it.

"We were all alone out here in the country when we started. Now we are surrounded by houses. There was a housing development that was practically empty. The sales manager came to me to say our people could buy houses. Now they are all sold. Tenants, those who were too late to buy, pay about $50 a month rent. If a woman makes $40 a week and her husband makes something, it all helps to pay the rent and give them a decent house to live in. Besides, Puerto Rican families group together. It's a Spanish custom. The families share their refrigerators, their televisions, and even their salaries. We had a man with two married sons and their wives all working here. On Friday they all took their pay envelopes to him.

"We try to offer our workers more than a job here. We offer them personal improvement and guidance. In the plant, in the hills, we keep constant contact with our workers. I myself, I live in the hills with the workers. Whenever a girl or a man marries, I enjoy going to the wedding. They're big Spanish weddings, the way they like them up in the hills. Mother's Day and Father's Day are big days here. They celebrate them in all their homes. I am invited to all of them and I go to as many as I can. At Christmas I couldn't invite 1,400 workers to my home, so I invited the workers who live within one kilometer of where I live. Last Christmas we had over one hundred guests; imagine one hundred workers living around my home. I see them Sundays at the church. I give them a lift on the road. I fill up the car to capacity."

To sophisticated labor-minded people, the image of a plant manager giving employees a lift in his car, or inviting them to his home, may sound somewhat like a plantation owner in the South protesting his love for his indentured servants. But Puerto Rico is an emerging democracy. This is a stage in the development of Puerto Rico's workers. In Latin tradition, most Puerto Ricans would rather work at lower wages for an employer who takes them shopping in his car, sits down with them occasionally, and asks them about their children than for an impersonal employer who pays them a

higher wage but who yells at them, watches them suspiciously to
see if perhaps they are stealing, and insults their sense of *"dignidad."* In a few years, Puerto Rican workers may develop greater
sophistication; they may want a less subjective relationship with
their employer. But it is typically Puerto Rican that both workers
and employers are aware that man does not live by bread alone.
In the climate of Puerto Rican industrialization, a Whittenton or a
Verdiales is exactly right.

It was Consolidated Cigar which originated the idea, now being
used in other plants, of placing advertisements in the Spanish newspapers in New York for homesick mechanics and toolmakers. Two
hundred Puerto Ricans answered the first ad. Verdiales interviewed
them all. In the plant itself, Verdiales placed a Puerto Rican in
charge of every department. This is company policy. Most of the
foremen were men in their thirties who had served in the Korean
War, where Puerto Ricans distinguished themselves for their
bravery. I talked to Pedro Santa, who had served in Korea and
Europe. "I studied at the University of Puerto Rico to be a teacher,"
Santa told me. "Then I worked in Chicago in a foundry for Inland
Steel and studied at the University of Chicago for two and a half
years."

"Why did you come back to Puerto Rico?" I asked him.

"I came back because this is my land. I like it. These are my
people. These are my customs. I was away too many times. I
wanted a job and I was lucky. Mr. Verdiales gave me a job. They
sent me to the mainland to be trained in a Consolidated Cigar factory. Now I rent a three-room house for $70 a month across the
road from the factory. We have four children. Two boys and two
girls. What do we have in our home? A TV, a refrigerator, a wash-
ing machine, a radio, and, of course, furniture. I have a '53 Chevy.
I started making 75 cents an hour. Now I earn almost $425 a
month. I might like to go to New York as a visitor, but not to work."

One of the newest and most exciting plants on the island is
Molinos de Puerto Rico (literally the Mills of Puerto Rico), a feed
and flour mill which looks like the Middle West on the Bay of San
Juan. It was started in typical Fomento manner. For five years
Fomento's economists made economic and feasibility studies in the

flour and feed program. They wanted a mill on the island to lower the cost and improve the quality of flour and animal feed. They knew that with animal feed produced locally at better values, their farmers could raise all the poultry the island people could eat, produce all their own eggs, increase the size of their hogs, and start a vitally needed beef cattle industry. It was not enough for the dreamers of the revolution to bring industry to the island for industry's sake, nor to give employment to the jobless. They wanted to use industry to make their people healthy, to change their food habits, to add proteins to their diet of rice and beans. Perhaps by 1975, the island could feed itself.

Fomento wrote letters all over the United States, suggesting to feed and flour companies that there were great advantages on the island. No one came. But Puerto Ricans believe in miracles. One day early in 1957, J. Allan Mactier, thirty-eight-year-old head of Nebraska Consolidated Mills took a vacation trip to Puerto Rico with his wife, to visit one of her schoolmates who had married and settled there. In San Juan he dropped in unannounced at the Fomento office at Stop 22, Santurce. As soon as Hu Barton and Moe Moses learned that he was a mill man, they started talking. Molinos de Puerto Rico was born.

Now in a seven-story milling plant, nearly two hundred employees are helping speed up the changing economy of the island. There are about a hundred millers and mechanics working with the brand-new machinery. In the flour and corn mills, pneumatic air tubes send the grains from the 50,000-bushel grain elevator over to the mill to be cleaned, milled, sifted, enriched, and packed in various-sized packages for delivery to the many bakeries all over the island. A completely automatic and modern feed mill, which is immediately adjacent to the flour mill, takes by-products from the flour mill and high-quality ingredients from other sources, mixes them into a high-energy animal and poultry feed for delivery to the farmers of the island.

Owen W. Cotton, the thirty-eight-year-old Executive Vice-President and General Manager of the Mills of Puerto Rico, a former midwestern farm boy who is also an executive in the parent company in Nebraska, talked straight from the shoulder. "Why did we come here," he asked, sitting behind a modernistic desk in his air-conditioned office. "We came here because it was economically sound. Puerto Rico has had all the saviors it could afford. We don't think it's evil to make a profit.

"To talk of Molinos in terms of tax exemption is distorting. Exemption is only ten years. This building will last a hundred years. Tax exemption just gold-plates your decision, if everything else is all right.

"We have built the most modern mill on the face of the earth right here. It's a pneumatic mill; no old-fashioned conveyors are used. We chose to build this plant here because there was a big market, there was a great source of labor, and what's very important, we could produce high-quality products at savings to the consumers. Sure, if Puerto Rico had not been part of the United States, it would have been a different picture. It's been expensive coming here. We invested three million dollars, and we borrowed $1,650,000 from the Government Development Bank of Puerto Rico. We'd like to get our investment back in five years.

"Some people say we've displaced certain employees. But the two hundred people we employ are more than any number of employees we displaced. You can't automate men out of the picture. I'm prouder of our men than I am of this building. Any fool can put up a building; anyone can put his mistakes into concrete. But the people—they're what count. We've found very little absenteeism. What we have found is that many don't want to work overtime or week ends. They want to spend week ends with their wives and families. As for people we bring from the States, we pay them 25% more than we do in the States. A man making $10,000 a year in the States gets $12,500 a year here. We're not giving him anything. He spends it on the higher cost of living."

Molinos has set up "Pig Palaces" to feed and fatten pigs. Molinos men go to any farmer who asks, build a "Pig Palace" for him, and teach him that his pigs should not walk off a pound of their meat. The palace is usually a thousand square feet. The farmer may bring the pig in at forty pounds, feed him with the new enriched Molinos feed, move him a little every two weeks, and in ten weeks he weighs two hundred pounds.

Now the "Pig Palaces" have created a need for another industry on the island—slaughtering houses. A large firm from Little Rock, Arkansas, is opening the Puerto Rican Meat Packing Company in Caguas. The slaughter house may change another aspect of life in Puerto Rico—roasting pigs on the spit. Before the slaughter houses, pigs were rarely grown beyond seventy-five pounds, in order to fit on a roasting spit. Now with slaughter houses and "Pig Palaces" they can be grown to two hundred and fifty pounds, and more. Farmers are being convinced not to slaughter their very young bulls as they had done for generations, but to raise them for expensive cuts.

The studies of Fomento's economists are paying off. The flour mill began a kind of industrial chain reaction. The slaughter house buys the feed to fatten the cattle whose hides are used for the leather industry, whose meat is used for a healthier population, whose meat scraps are sold back to Molinos to make more feed. Breweries buy brewers' grits, make brewers' grain, and sell back the spent grain to the mill. Tuna canneries sell fish scraps for feed. Puerto Rico is now becoming a fish-packing center. The tuna fisheries for years fished off the coast of Peru and sent the fish to California. But new fishing areas have now been discovered off the coast of Africa which are much closer to Puerto Rico than they are to California. So tuna packers like Star Kist Company are now building plants on the island to join Van Camp.

Supermarkets have come to Puerto Rico and, like Molinos, have helped change not only the rice-and-bean diet habits of the people, but have cut the price of food. Young thirty-five-year-old Harold Toppel who was in the supermarket business in New Jersey, came to Puerto Rico on a week-end vacation in March 1952, saw the island's potential, sold out in New Jersey, returned in 1954, and now, with his two older brothers, operates six Pueblo supermarkets in San Juan and Ponce, with plans for others already on the boards.

Studies made for the United States Civil Service Commission show that the cost of living for Federal Government employees working in Puerto Rico is 17% higher than in Washington, D. C. This reflects the higher cost of apartment rentals, English-language schools, automobiles, and other transportation costs. It leaves out of account such local benefits as inexpensive household help. The Federal Government has just reduced the cost of living differential paid to civil servants working in Puerto Rico from 17% to 12½%.

Many people have attributed the higher cost of living to the mark-up on food. Toppel refutes this. "In our prices," he said, "we follow the formula for mark-ups in the States. So our prices are really the same as in the stateside supermarkets, except that we have to pay freight for bringing them here. That brings up the cost about 10%.

"Some things we sell cheaper than in the States. Puerto Rico is the highest purchaser per capita, in the world, of tomato sauce. Last year, 1,800,000 cases of tomato sauce were sold in Puerto Rico in a population of 2,300,000 people. The small eight-ounce cans of tomato sauce in New York generally sell for 9.2 cents a can or about four cans for 37 cents. We sell four cans for 33 cents, or 8.2 cents a can. Salt, another big item here, sells for 11 or 12 cents a box in New York. We sell the same brand for 9 cents. Sugar in the States costs 49 cents for a five-pound bag. We sell it for 47 cents because we can buy it locally from a sugar refinery in Ponce; it's called 'Snow-White' brand."

Certainly before the supermarkets opened, food prices were exorbitant. Every wholesale distributor could blame the high price he charged on transportation and scarcity. The Pueblo supermarkets, followed by the Rockefellers who built the Todos supermarkets and sold them to Grand Union in 1959, ended the monopoly.

Large shopping centers are being built all over the island, with supermarkets, dress shops, and even branches of chain stores, such as Woolworth, Kresge, and Sears Roebuck, opening in various places. Oil companies are drilling for oil. Refineries have already been set up.

Much of the food imported from the States is now brought in on Pan-Atlantic Steamship Company's trailer trucks. This is a new "lift-on, lift-off" service. Food and other products are loaded from warehouses in the States into a van placed on a trailer-truck, which is sealed and driven to the loading dock. Here special cranes on the "trailer-ships," freighters that have been converted to hold the sealed vans, lift each van up in two minutes and deposit it inside

The Commonwealth Oil Refinery at Guayanilla, near Ponce

the vertical rails of a cell. All over the island now one sees the new
Fomento-aided industries shipping their products back to the States
in these sealed "piggy-back" trailers.

"Bootstrap" has changed the face of Puerto Rico. Fomento is
the chief architect of that change. Now Fomento has set its sights
on the year 1975. By then it hopes that 2,500 new factories will
have settled on the island to employ 256,000 people directly
and create a similar number of secondary jobs. The sparkling new
Fomento buildings will dot the landscape—modern, spotlessly
clean, with men and women rooted to their soil, able to send their
children to school, to clothe them and feed them and house them
decently. Fomento's new industries will thus not only be creating
jobs for Puerto Ricans, but giving them the chance to stay home
on the island they love.

CHAPTER 6

They Walk with Pride

Don Fernando Sierra Berdecía is the Secretary of Labor, a playwright, journalist, columnist and, in this labor-minded government, one of the philosophers of the revolution.

Both Don Fernando, the official representative of labor, and Teodoro Moscoso, the head of Fomento, are leaders. Both are Puerto Ricans. Yet each is, in a sense, typical of one of the two profiles of the island. The image of Moscoso is of an American executive; he is called like a mainlander by his last name, or familiarly, Ted; but almost never Don Teodoro. The Secretary of Labor is always Don Fernando, or, more formally, Señor Sierra Berdecía.

Moscoso speaks English like a New Yorker; Don Fernando has a soft-spoken Spanish accent. Moscoso was graduated from the University of Michigan in 1932, where he studied pharmacy, but by voracious reading and an extraordinary memory has turned himself into a first-rate industrialist and economist who reads modern Italian novels for relaxation. Don Fernando is a former bohemian, a romantic philosopher who not only administers a huge department but writes plays and columns about the problems of the island and the people who migrate.

He himself has been a migrant and a returnee. His was the

pattern of Puerto Rico's young intellectuals in the twenties. In 1922 as a high school student, he joined the little group of students who organized the Nationalist Party. But he soon withdrew in protest against their would-be terrorism.

"My grandmother, with whom I grew up, died," he told me. "It was in 1923. I was facing economic problems. I was twenty years old and I went to New York to study and work. New York was the golden land, the promised land. But I found it hard to work. I was a dishwasher, a cashier in a restaurant, a house-man in a hotel, cleaning windows. Meanwhile I was writing articles and sending them back to Puerto Rico."

His life paralleled Muñoz'. They met with other Puerto Rican intellectuals in a cafeteria in Greenwich Village or one on 110th Street. New York was to the young Puerto Rican rebels what Paris was to Hemingway and the coterie around Gertrude Stein. But the Puerto Ricans were not art for art's sake rebels; they were not expatriates. Their writing was political and polemical. They wanted the world to know of the crime of Puerto Rico, of colonialism even under the United States.

In 1926, Don Fernando returned to the island and worked as a reporter on Muñoz' paper, *La Democracia*. In 1930 he joined with Muñoz in the newly organized Liberal Party. He worked on various newspapers and in 1938 left the Liberal Party with Muñoz to become one of the architects of the Popular Democratic Party. After the elections of 1940, he was made Secretary to the Minimum Wage Board in the Labor Department. In 1947 he was appointed Commissioner of Labor, and has remained the head of the Labor Department.

He is probably the only Secretary of Labor who has had one of his own plays produced while in office. In the summer of 1959, the Theatre Festival in San Juan produced *"Esta Noche Juega El Joker"*—"The Joker Plays Tonight." Its hero, a Puerto Rican, migrates to New York and falls in love with a beautiful woman who is more successful than he is. To keep her love he does things incredible for a traditional Puerto Rican with Spanish pride—he begins to cook and sweep and clean the house. The play examines the new status of women, the dilemma of the newcomers from

A worker at the Cabo Rojo salt works on the west coast

Latin America in New York, and ends happily as the hero adjusts to his Americanized role.

The Secretary of Labor has never given up journalism. He writes a column for *El Mundo,* the newspaper which advocates statehood. Yet in its columns Don Fernando, politically and philosophically in opposition, fully discusses why he believes statehood would be disastrous for Puerto Rico. Freedom of the press is no shibboleth in Puerto Rico. It is in the very fabric of the land.

You can joke with Don Fernando. You can listen to his poetry and his plays. You can swap stories with him through half the night. But beneath the artist and the writer and the lover of good music you know that there is a first-rate administrator who has fought every moment for the rights of labor. So important is labor on this island that Don Fernando is perhaps the "second-best-known" man in the country, second only to the Governor himself.

During Don Fernando's administration, the Puerto Rican worker has won new status on the island. His wages have risen steadily. His standard of living has come up. He can pay for decent housing. His children can go to school. He walks with pride.

"We had two problems when we started in the forties," Don Fernando told me one day in his home in Santa María, an attractive upper-middle-class neighborhood in San Juan. We were eating a typically Puerto Rican Sunday dinner of chicken, rice and beans, and fresh salad, prepared by his tall quiet-spoken wife. His grandchildren were playing on the terrace.

"We needed to create employment and we needed to raise the standard of living. That's why two courses were developed by the government—one, the Industrial Program with tax exemption, and two, the Labor Department program with minimum wages, promoting collective bargaining between organized labor and management.

"The basic philosophy of the Labor Department," Don Fernando went on, "is to raise the standard of living of all our people. We have to industrialize the land but we don't want to do it just to help a group of industrialists. We want to distribute, in the most democratic and adequate way, all the benefits of industry—increased wages and increased productivity too. You develop purchasing power among workers so the good products which the workers make can be sold."

We talked of the ever-present fear that if wages go up too sharply, the Fomento industries might shut down. The minimum wage in some industries is already a dollar an hour.

"Wages should go up to keep pace with the cost of living," Don Fernando said, "and to see that the social profits of industry are properly distributed among the whole community and do not stay in the hands of a few. Of course we're concerned that if wages go up unrealistically, breaking out of bounds of the normal economic expansion of the island, some of the Fomento industries could close down.

"In the wage area we cannot as yet compete with the Southern states, but we can already compete in other areas. We can develop productivity. It's difficult to measure labor productivity, but many employers have told us that the Puerto Rican workers have very great productivity, and in some industries we have greater productivity than in the United States, in the South or even in the North."

Almost every employer I met praised the productivity of the island's workers. "As workers they are just about as good as workers in the States," Joe Fox, the general manager and treasurer of the International Molded Plastics of Puerto Rico, Inc. in Carolina, told me one day. One hundred men and women were making plastic dishes, working the large modern machines in the brightly lighted plant.

"We have some people here I would call 'very superior,' " he said, "like our plant superintendent, John Gotos, who has originality and has given us some first-rate ideas in manufacturing. I've found it a little more difficult to get good maintenance people, but everyone else is good. In fact George Goulder, the president of our parent firm in Cleveland, took movies of the people working on the line here. He showed the movies in Cleveland to the employees. They refused to believe he hadn't speeded up the film."

The patron saint of labor is Santiago Iglesias. Early in the 1900's Iglesias went to Washington where he met Samuel Gompers who, recognizing his ability, appointed him the island's chief organizer for the American Federation of Labor. Iglesias founded the Free Federation of Workers, the insular branch of the A. F. of L., and began the process of affiliating many Puerto Rican unions with the international unions on the mainland. He became a voice of influence throughout Latin America, and as head of the Puerto Rican Socialist Party in the 1920's, helped mold Muñoz' early identification with labor. In 1932 the Socialists joined forces with the Republicans in a coalition and Iglesias was elected Puerto Rico's Resident Commissioner to Washington. He died in office on December 5, 1939.

Girls in a pineapple canning factory near Manati on the north coast

Today the Fomento plants are covetously eyed by union organizers, locally and from the mainland. A heated battle is being waged between James Hoffa's Teamsters Union and other international unions, particularly Paul Hall's Seafarers International Union, which grew in the first six months of 1959 from 400 to 1,500 members.

Hoffa's union has succeeded in organizing some six companies, among them the drivers and printers in *El Mundo*. The story circulating on the island is that when Hoffa sent men and money to Puerto Rico in 1958, *El Mundo* printed vitriolic articles describing Hoffa's alleged malpractices then being investigated by the Select Senate Committee on Improper Labor-Management Activities. The articles portrayed Hoffa as so evil that the paper's truck drivers decided, "If the boss thinks Hoffa's so bad there must be something good about him." They voted overwhelmingly to join the Teamsters Union.

Even hard-boiled mainland unions take on a Puerto Rican flavor when they organize on the island. At a regular monthly meeting in the Seafarers Union labor hall in San Juan, as some two hundred workers sat listening to their president's report on the battle with Hoffa, exotic birds sang in a large cage, multicolored tropical fish swam in a huge aquarium, and large tropical plants brought the Puerto Rican landscape right into the union meeting.

The government is pro-labor, and the Constitution of the Commonwealth guarantees workers the legal right to organize. A man or woman is free to join a union or work in an open shop. This is a democratic country. But the government leaders say frankly they would like to see mainland unions which they consider "socially responsible" come down to the island. Among the international unions already in Puerto Rico are the United Packing House Workers of America, which organized the farm workers in the sugar *centrales* and now has the largest membership on the island; the International Union of Electrical Workers; the Amalgamated Clothing Workers of America; the International Longshoremen's Association; the United Brewery, Distillery and Tobacco Workers of America; the United Rubber, Cork, Linoleum and Plastic Workers of America; and the International Ladies' Garment Workers Union whose Local 600 has a membership of nearly 5,000.

A few years ago David Dubinsky, President of the ILGWU. illustrated what socially responsible labor leaders were doing. Dubinsky, in 1956, actually fought *against* hiking wages for brassiere workers on the island.

Brassieres are big business in Puerto Rico. One out of every five brassieres sold in the United States is made in Puerto Rico. Many famous brassiere companies, Maidenform, Exquisite Form, Peter Pan, Lady Marlene, and others, have factories on the island. In 1955, the legal minimum wage for all continental brassiere workers was raised to $1.00. Early in 1956, in Puerto Rico, where minimums in each industry are individually reviewed by federal boards, the legal minimum for brassiere workers was raised from 55 to 70 cents an hour and, under the terms of the first union contract, to 75 cents along with several fringe benefits. Soon afterward, the Puerto Rico House of Representatives proposed an amendment to boost the minimum for brassiere workers to $1.00 to match the States. But David Dubinsky stood up on the floor of the ILGWU convention, then in session in Atlantic City, and denounced the amendment as premature. He was convinced that the insular brassiere industry could not yet afford such a hike in wages. If they moved out of Puerto Rico, the workers would again be unemployed.

"I am fully cognizant," he told the convention, "of my responsibilities as a labor leader, as a friend of Puerto Rico, and as a representative of the workers of Puerto Rico. I want them to have a decent wage, and I want them to have work, but I do not want them to have a wage without work. . . . We want a minimum wage without politics. We do not want a political minimum."

Unemployment is still a serious problem on the island. A development program like Fomento's, while it gives jobs to many people, basically does not solve unemployment. Fomento has upgraded many jobs, but it has also eliminated through mechanization and skills many of the marginal jobs, particularly in agriculture and in needlework. The new industrialization has considerably reduced partial employment, which has long plagued the island. When the main industries were the seasonal ones—sugar, coffee, tobacco—people worked in the season, and then starved. Now the new industries employ workers 40 to 50 weeks during the year. Still the number of unemployed is high.

In 1949 there were 214,000 workers employed in agriculture. In 1959 there were only 137,000. Puerto Rico's labor force is now close to 600,000 people; yet there is an average unemployment of 13 to 15% of that number. Some 85,000 are still unemployed. The figure is better than it was ten years ago when 100,000 were unemployed, but these improved statistics have little meaning to a man who is hungry.

Unemployment compensation, which was paid for the first time on January 1, 1959, pays between $7 and $12 a week for a maximum period of seven weeks during the year. To be sure, this is only the beginning, but it is scarcely enough to keep a family alive if a plant shuts down.

All over the island, when word spreads that a firm is looking for workers, hundreds of people turn up before the doors open. They may have walked for miles down the hills, or driven for hours in buses and *públicos*—public taxis. These are not necessarily unskilled people, though to be sure there are many unskilled among them. Some are high school and college graduates, teachers, nurses, dietitians, technicians. But in the hospitals, for example, they may have been earning $27 a week. Now word spreads that salaries in the factories are $31 a week, perhaps even $40, and everyone comes looking.

A warm-hearted private secretary in one of the large electronic plants told me that she nearly wept whenever her firm advertised for a handful of workers. "They would be lined up even before I came to work," she said. "They would show me their empty pocket books. Their feet were sore from walking. I would tell them there is no work. But they would hang around all day in the hope that some miracle would happen. Some of them would say, 'I have relatives in New York who want me to come. They want to send me money for the airplane. But I want to work here. This is my home.' In recent years many were returning from the States. 'We got good pay there but it was cold and I wanted to go home.' "

Migration is inevitable. Economists hope that by 1975 there may be enough work to end the chronic unemployment. But today everyone on the island realizes that there must be an exodus so long as the population keeps exploding, and each year more job seekers grow of age.

"We don't encourage or discourage migration to the States," Don Fernando told me, explaining the policy of the Commonwealth. "But we think that if there were no migration, there would be a much higher unemployment.

"In a sense, we are discouraging migration by promoting new industries. We are encouraging skilled workers to stay or come back to the island. We want to develop this island in such a way that whoever is born here and whoever wants to come and live with us,

A worker on a sugar farm near Lajas on the southwestern tip of the island

will not have to leave because he has no job. But we want him to
have complete freedom to choose whatever he does."

Meanwhile seasonal migratory work has helped give employment
to thousands of Puerto Ricans who do not want to break their
ties with the island for more than a few months at a time. Each year
about 20,000 agricultural workers travel from Puerto Rico to pick
crops in Florida, New Jersey, Connecticut, New York, and other
states for a few months and then return to the island and their
families. These are no "Okies" left on their own. These are no
vagrants to be exploited. They leave the island only after a contract is signed by their employers under the laws of the State and

the Commonwealth. Before they go, Puerto Rican Labor Department officials must approve the wages offered, the housing facilities,
and the working conditions.

Puerto Rico is the only government in the world which follows
its workers to the States, whether they are seasonal or permanent
migrants, and continues to look after them through its Migration
Division. The Labor Department has now begun a *"Programa de
Orientación"*—a program of orientation for potential migrants.

Each worker is given a series of pamphlets entitled: "You in the
United States." The first pamphlet is called "It is Necessary to
Learn English." Another suggests how to dress in the States; and
one of the most interesting asks the question, *"Me Voy O Me
Quedo"*—"Shall I Go or Shall I Stay?"

A woman heads up this crucially important Migration Division.
She is Petroamérica Pagán de Colón, or as she is known affectionately all over the island, Petro, a vivacious woman with black hair
pinned into a bun, shining black eyes, and, like most Puerto Rican
women, completely feminine. She was given her unique name,
Petroamérica, by her father, who took the name of her two grandmothers, Petra, changed it to Petro, and added the name of the
country he loved.

In the Labor Department, Petroamérica is Don Fernando's right
hand. The eleven offices of the Migration Division in the States are
her responsibility. It is to these offices, whether they are in New
York, Chicago, or New England, that many Puerto Ricans come
to inquire about an apartment, schools, scholarships for gifted children, and most important of all, a job.

Petro travels almost as much as Eleanor Roosevelt, making constant trips back and forth from the island to the States, speaking,
meeting with Puerto Rican communities, helping them adjust.

Fortunately, her family is an understanding one. Her husband,
Juan A. Colón, is a judge who holds court all over the island. They
have two sons, Juan Rafael, known familiarly as Papo, who is
studying medicine at the University of Puerto Rico, and Frankie,
now thirteen, who wants to be a lawyer like his father.

You cannot really understand a Puerto Rican woman unless you
see her in the midst of her family. Petro, an efficient housekeeper

Mrs. Petroamérica Pagán de Colón, head of the Migration Division's
Orientation Program, seeing off seasonal farm workers to the States

and cook, runs her home like a Grand Central Station for visitors
from the States and for people who ask her help.

Her whole life was a preparation for her job as a top labor
official. She was graduated from the University of Puerto Rico, with
an A.B. in education, did postgraduate work in sociology at Columbia University, became a principal of a public school and then
Director of the Bureau of Vocational Rehabilitation in San Juan. In
1948, she joined the Department of Labor, and today heads up its
huge Bureau of Employment Security.

Organized labor on the island is now a lusty, brawling child,
becoming more aware each day of its own strength. It is typical of
the new Puerto Rico that one of its top labor officials is a woman.

CHAPTER 7

The Mayor of San Juan
Is a Mayoress

Every Wednesday morning Doña Felisa, the Mayoress of San Juan, holds open house at the City Hall. It is *"El Día de Entrevistas,"* the Day of the Interviews, when petitioners come to their Mayoress from all parts of her city.

By 7:00 o'clock one sunny morning, some three hundred people had already assembled in the huge Council Chamber of San Juan's historic City Hall. The seats were arranged like a theatre; and the people, dressed in their Sunday best, sat quietly, waiting with eagerness, curiosity, and tense emotion for the curtain to rise.

At 9:00 Doña Felisa entered, a large woman with a cameo-like face, wearing a freshly starched beige linen dress and long jacket, her white hair—her mark of distinction—fixed in two huge buns tied with a black ribbon. She sat at a desk facing the people. The desk was bare save for two small pads of white paper and a cluster of blue-colored pencils. The pad was the magic link between Doña Felisa and the solution to the people's problems. She had only to write the letter "F" on the pad and doors opened all over the city.

A chair was placed at her right side and here each petitioner sat for a minute, five minutes, or as long as he needed. Doña Felisa

Doña Felisa, Mayoress of San Juan, writing a note on her pad
for one of her petitioners in front of the Municipal Hospital

listened, her face filled with interest or compassion, never with
censure. She nodded her head, then wrote a word or two on her pad.
On many she wrote *"Mira a ver. F"* (Look and see. Felisa). A
social worker took the person to the door and told him to which
government agency to go. Some of the requests, of course, required
a thorough investigation. But many were for shoes for children,
and for these Doña Felisa wrote simply on her magic pad *"1 par."*

Her people obviously expected Doña Felisa to be everything—
from a legal counsel to a one-woman court of human relations.
One woman, sitting hopefully at her side, said, "Doña Felisa, my
husband hasn't shown up for three days. If you will come to dinner
at my house, he will hear about it and he will come home."

Doña Felisa went to dinner and the truant husband returned.

As each person walked toward the Mayoress, the entire audience stood up and moved one seat closer to her desk as though they were playing a game of musical chairs. Suddenly a man in the front row became hysterical. He coughed and choked. His skin turned a purplish gray. Two officials led him out of the room while Doña Felisa continued holding open house. Ten minutes later one of the men came back to report. "He's better now. We can take care of everything he wants. But he insists he must see you."

Doña Felisa nodded.

The man returned quietly to his seat, the hysteria completely under control. When his turn came, he sat next to her. She put her graceful fingers on his work-worn hand.

"My wife died," he said. "Then my shack fell down completely. They promised to fix it for me. But they didn't. Now I have nowhere to live."

Doña Felisa gave him the magic slip to be taken to her construction people in charge of repairing old shacks. "Come see me urgently. F." She wanted to be certain that his story was true.

Just touching her hand healed some of the people. Just to be able to talk to her was therapy enough.

She is the mother image of San Juan. She is the safety valve for pent-up emotions. She is a combination of Louis XIV, a twentieth-century Lady Bountiful, and a female La Guardia running a city of more than half a million.

I first met Doña Felisa in 1949 on Three Kings Day, the "Twelfth Night" after Christmas. She had been mayoress for three years; and she had already discovered the road to the heart of San Juan's people. Some fourteen thousand children and parents had assembled in the bleachers of the Sixto Escobar Stadium, with the excitement and suspense of a World Series game. Entertainers kept the crowd happy. Vendors sold soft drinks and *pasteles* (meat wrapped in banana leaves). And whole groups of the city's poorest children walked, in orderly fashion, to their mayoress who stood in the midst of sacks of toys, like a Lady Santa Claus.

Each year the numbers of children grew until it became physically impossible for Doña Felisa to give toys to over fifty thousand

Men dressed as the Three Kings, Gaspar, Melchior,
and Balthasar, in the courtyard of La Fortaleza

children in the stadium. Now, early in the fall, leaders in the slums send cards to each family. The people are told on what day to appear at City Hall for their children's toys. Meanwhile Doña Felisa has been busy for months writing personal letters to business organizations, asking them to contribute to the toy fund. On the second or third day of December, the parents begin coming to City Hall for the toys. Doña Felisa admonishes them to hide the toys until January 6th in a secure place, and to tell their children that the gifts have come, not from City Hall but from the Three Kings.

I shared some of her days with her. She started one typical day at 6:00 in the morning. Her chauffeur drove her around San Juan

Doña Felisa distributing toys for Three Kings' Day

to see if the street cleaners were cleaning the streets and the garbage collectors were collecting garbage.

At 8:00 she was back in her huge office in City Hall, whose main entrance is three hundred and fifty years old. Her huge brown wooden desk, with green felt and a glass top, was already neatly piled with papers. Behind her desk hung the Great Seal of San Juan, with a lamb and the letters F and I, for Ferdinand and Isabella. At her left stood three flags: the flag of the United States, the red, white, and blue flag of the Commonwealth with a white star in a field of blue, and the flag of her city, San Juan Bautista de Puerto Rico, brilliantly orange with the Great Seal in the center.

Her first conference was at 8:00 to discuss a new parking place for the booming city. At 10:00 she hurried over to *El Imparcial* to help inaugurate a new rotary press. At 11:00 she rushed back to City Hall to give a reception for ten different groups of visitors to the island, among them an engineer from the Hashemite Kingdom of Jordan and Dr. Joseph O. Loretan, Associate Superintendent of Schools of New York City's Board of Education.

At lunch, ten of us sat at a long conference table in her office and toasted the guest of honor, the lady Minister of Education from Costa Rica, with typical Puerto Rican wishes: *"Pesetas para gastarlas. Y salud para gozarlas"* (Money to spend, and health to enjoy it).

There were short speeches. Doña Felisa gave the gold key of the city to the Costa Rican Minister, and to the others she gave silk replicas of the three flags near her desk.

At 2:00 the Chief of Police and some of his assistants dropped in. At 3:00 she had a meeting to discuss an indoor food market at Río Piedras with the city engineers and some of the workers. At 4:00 she changed her clothes, fixed her hair-do into a silver braid which she wore like a crown, and attended another reception for *El Imparcial* at the Normandie Hotel. At 7:00 she was at a party at the French Consulate and at 9:00 was being ushered into the home of José Benítez, then President of the Committee of the Democratic Party of Puerto Rico. It is essentially a paper party, with barely three hundred members. It has not yet been registered as a party and most Democrats vote with the Popular Party.

I know few mayors on the mainland who control their city as completely as Doña Felisa controls hers and at the same time inspire such love. I have watched barefoot women kiss the hem of her dress. Some have burst into song. "Felisa, Felisa has come to see us." Throughout the city, children catching sight of her in the car, shout familiarly, "Fela, Fela."

One afternoon we drove through the slums of San Juan with another woman political leader, Doña Josefina O. de Battle, the vice-chairman of the Board of Commissioners, a petite, red-haired woman with amber eyes.

From stately-looking Loíza Street, a main thoroughfare with beautiful homes and gardens burgeoning with tropical flowers, we turned into an obscure narrow alley and entered another world.

The shacks, built up above the mud on planks, were in various stages of collapse. Some of the houses were termite-ridden boards nailed together. Open rivers of sewage ran between the shacks. The air was filled with the smell of foul water and garbage.

Yet inside the open doors, the shacks were clean. Men and

Moving out of a slum in San Juan

women, hearing excitement in the alley, rushed to their glassless windows to greet their two women leaders with outbursts of joy.

Doña Josefina led the way. She was the political leader of the ward. She had brought Doña Felisa to her barrio to help some of the people rebuild their houses and their lives. We stopped at a shack that looked like a wooden cave. A young woman stepped out, barefoot. She wore an old housedress and a bandanna on her head. She held a naked baby tightly in her arms. Six more children tumbled out of the shack.

"For two years," the young mother told us, "we've been living here without a drop of water or light. Now even the house is falling to the ground. Please help us, Doña Felisa."

"I will help," Doña Felisa said, and wrote a little note on her pad.

As we walked through the alley, stepping gingerly on planks across the streams of refuse, Doña Felisa told me, "The housing people tell me I should burn down these slums immediately. I want the people out. I want them in the new projects. But before new

Moving into a new low-cost housing project, the Luis
Llorens Torres housing development in San Juan

projects go up—what shall we do? Put the people in the streets?
You are always dealing with people, with human beings, with lives.

"In ten years," she went on, "these slums will all disappear.
Meanwhile we help them. My construction men help them rebuild
their houses with the wood of their shacks, if the termites haven't
eaten it too badly. Or we give them new material. And paint.
Houses. Houses. Houses. This is our main problem. And money.
This barrio is living right on a sewer. Now we have started a sewage
project here. It costs half a million dollars."

An ancient Negro woman with an aristocratic face and body,
bare feet with talon-like toenails, and a ragged skirt and blouse welcomed us into her home. She showed us how most of her ceiling
had disintegrated, and how the rains, which come suddenly and
fiercely, had flooded her house.

In another shack a smiling young woman offered us food and
cold drinks. Three families with all their children were living in
two tiny rooms for which they paid their landlord $12 a month
rent. The young woman, with simple dignity, said to her Mayoress,

"Doña Felisa for $12 a month we could live in a decent apartment in a housing project. But we can't get into one. Maybe you could help us?"

This was a hard request. The housing projects were already filled to overflowing. "But we'll keep on building more and more. You'll get there," Doña Felisa said.

We left to visit another San Juan slum, the barrio of San Ciprian. Scarcely two years ago, no car could drive through it. You walked on planks, or waded through the mud and sewage. Now the city engineers were putting the houses on caterpillar trucks and moving them into rows to make way for a street on which cars could drive. But the houses themselves were shacks in which it was hard to imagine human beings could live. Buzzards hovered over them, as though the smell of death were in the air.

These were rat-infested, vulture-ridden breeding places of disease and prostitution, of assault and pilferage. Here was the Puerto Rico that had not yet moved up out of the degradation of the depression years and the ruin that came in the wake of the big hurricanes of 1928 and 1932, which almost wrecked the island's economy. Yet despite the utter deprivation, the people kept their strength. Even in the lowliest shack, you felt the drive to stay alive. They had faith —faith that something would happen, that they would ultimately move out of this nightmare alley, that Doña Felisa would help.

"This is my life," Doña Felisa said to me as we walked around the slum. She was followed like a pied piper by dozens of little urchins. "This is why I work three hundred and sixty-five days a year."

"Hi, Felisa," a little boy called in English. "How're things?"

"Hi," she answered in English, and took his hand. "Where did you learn your English? In the school here?"

"No," he said proudly, while the other boys listened curiously. "I lived in New York. But now I learn it in school too."

A school had been built right inside this slum, so that no child had an excuse for not learning.

Nearby, the city had built a large modern dispensary which took care of at least thirteen thousand children a month. The slum-dwellers were given free medical and dental care. As Doña Felisa

Inside the utter deprivation, the people keep their strength

walked through the clinic, women patients applauded. Their faces broke into smiles. Some embraced her. Some kissed her. Dozens followed her with requests. She listened patiently to each one, and wrote little notes in her pad.

"They come to me with confidence," she told me one night at dinner in the old Spanish patio of the City Hall. "They know that when I promise something, I keep my promise. They have faith. That is the important thing."

Some of her critics say that she is too much of a politician—that she is using old-fashioned Tammany Hall techniques in cementing her position and building her political machine. Some of the men in her own Popular Democratic Party are said to be scared to death of her, knowing the power she wields in her city of 600,000.

Yet, unique as she is, she fits into the tradition of mayors on the island. For centuries under the Spaniards the local mayor was the father, the social worker, the job counselor, the man-of-all-help. To this day, the mayors do the welfare job in their towns. Since they don't have to spend their time policing their cities—the Police and Fire Departments are under the Commonwealth—they have time to do a person-to-person job.

From Mayor José Barceló in Adjuntas high in the mountains in the middle of the island to the men of the coastal towns, every mayor I met had a room filled with petitioners who wanted help in finding housing, jobs, medical care, truant husbands or wives. In Mayagüez, I attended a quiet funeral wake in City Hall. The body of a distinguished widow had been brought from New York and her family wanted the services in a place of honor. Mayor Baudilio Vega Berrios gave them the City Hall.

Since San Juan is the largest city on the island, Doña Felisa's influence is greater than that of any other mayor. She has an amazing capacity to reach people. In relating to people, she has perfect pitch.

She can be elegant and formal; and she can be as gay as a giggling schoolgirl. She is a deeply religious Catholic, with strong friendships among people of all faiths. She can be frivolous at a carnival, and flirtatious behind her ever-present swiftly moving fan. She has a whole collection of fans that she has picked up all around the Spanish-speaking world.

In her beach home at Vega Baja, surrounded by her young nieces and nephews, she is as relaxed and informal as the most permissive grandmother. Lying on a sofa on the porch overlooking the ocean, she holds her husband's hand as though she had just announced her engagement to him.

Her childhood friends tell me that in their games Doña Felisa was always the mother. Though they never suspected the qualities which developed as she grew in her job, they were prepared for her mothering a whole city as she had once mothered her motherless family, her friends, and their dolls.

Doña Felisa was born January 9, 1897, in Ceiba, on the east coast of the island, and grew up in Humacao. Her father, Enrique Rincón Plumey, of Spanish and French heritage, was a lawyer. Her mother, Rita Marrero Rivera, also of Spanish descent, a school-teacher, died when Felisa was eleven, and the child became the mother of her family. True to the Puerto Rican tradition that the eldest child leaves school so that the younger ones can be educated, Felisa left high school until her sisters and brothers were graduated. Then she returned and studied pharmacy. But she quit to open a shop selling the hand embroidery for which the women of the island were famous. Later she opened a dress shop in San Juan and traveled to New York three or four times a year on buying trips.

She became a Puerto Rican suffragette. If women could vote, she thought, they might help alleviate some of the misery and hunger of Puerto Rico's sweatshop workers.

It was Manuel García Méndez, a lawyer and sugar plantation owner in Aguadilla, who introduced the bill in 1929 to grant women the right to vote. "Until that year," he told me, "women in Puerto Rico were in the same category as minors, beggars, idiots, and jailbirds. A drunkard or a moron could vote, but women in the University of Puerto Rico, novelists, writers, could not."

When suffrage was granted to women in 1932, Doña Felisa became a power in the politics of the island. She helped form the Popular Democratic Party in 1938, and soon became president of the Party Committee of San Juan, a position she still holds.

In 1940, Jenaro A. Gautier, a lawyer and one of the leaders of the Popular Democratic Party, recognized Felisa's innate political ability. He became her first political adviser and then her husband. Doña Felisa became Felisa Rincón de Gautier.

San Juan has a city management government, with thirteen com-missioners, seven elected and six appointed by the governor. Doña Felisa, appointed by the governor, was made Mayoress of San Juan in 1946.

San Juan was then a city of 250,000 people, with areas of great beauty and squalid slums. Doña Felisa set out with a big broom.

She made the people plant flowers and shrubs all over the city. Signs were put up on garbage trucks saying, "Help keep our city beautiful."

Street cleaners and garbage collectors were given status. One Sunday morning I drove with Doña Felisa to a meeting of the Independent Union of Street Cleaners and Garbage Collectors. On land that had a few years ago been unusable swamps at the edge of El Fanguito, the city government had built a huge "Public Works Center," a modernistic garage with repair shops, lockers, and showers for the men.

Right inside the Center, the city had built a meeting hall so the union could hold its meetings free. About two hundred men were already assembled, dressed in white shirts or freshly ironed plaid shirts. The president, José Nevarez, was speaking into a portable hand microphone as we entered. A dozen men sat on the platform. Large photos of Governor Muñoz Marín and of Doña Felisa, looking beautiful and regal in black lace, hung on the wall behind the speakers. The flag of the Commonwealth of Puerto Rico and the flag of the United States stood at opposite ends of the platform.

This was a union meeting but politics was the issue. The meeting was called to elect new officers and to inform the men of the benefits the union had obtained for them.

The president of the union said forcefully, "Under Governor Muñoz and Doña Felisa, under the Popular Democratic Party, labor is fully recognized in Puerto Rico. The other party that was in power before 1940, never even permitted us to have a union. They did nothing for us."

Doña Felisa applauded as enthusiastically as the workers. Nevarez now introduced her.

"My dear friends in work," she began, "when we started there was one uncovered garage and five uncovered trucks to clean our whole city. There were no warehouses and no machine shops with spare parts. Now we have spent thousands of dollars in warehouses, repair shops, and spare parts just to clean the streets.

"When I became mayor in 1946, most of you earned $1.20 a day. You had no vacations and you were paid your salary every five or six months. Many of you had to send your checks to a moneylender to be able to get some money to feed your wives and your children. There was no equipment for you then. No gloves, no uniforms. (Now the city gives each man gloves and four uniforms free.) You were called by the people, with great disdain, *'barren-deros'* (garbage collectors) and your morale was very low. Now garbage collectors earn $5.40 a day. Drivers make $200.00 a month, two-weeks' vacation with pay and two weeks' sick leave. Now you are proud employees of the city government.

"I remember when I used to take care of my own house; when I finished I would sit in a rocking chair and look around with pride. So I want you to take pride in what you are doing. When you clean a part of the city look around you with pride."

The men nodded appreciatively. Some clapped their hands above their head with approval. Every garbage collector and street cleaner in that union hall knew that the Government of Puerto Rico and the Mayoress of San Juan were on their side.

Whatever the future politics of the island may be, San Juan's lady mayor will have left her mark on the capital city for all time.

CHAPTER 8

"Now I Have My House"

In the summer of 1959, a three-way festival took place in the little village of Jayuya (pronounced Ha-YOU-Yah) high in the mountains in the interior of the island.

Early on a bright Sunday morning, a caravan of cars carrying the Governor and top officials in the Department of Agriculture, set out from La Fortaleza. Mayors and political leaders drove from all the towns around Jayuya, from Utuado on the river Río Grande de Arecibo, from Adjuntas with its magnificent tobacco fields and its rugged mountains called *Sillas de Calderón,* the Chairs of Calderon, and *El Gigante,* the Giant, carved by time into a giant's face. The jíbaros drove or came on horseback from all the hills.

For on this day, seventy landless farmers—*agregados*—were to draw lots for land. Forty-seven farmers were to draw lots for cows. And thirty-one families who had worked in teams building their own houses were to receive their certificates of ownership.

It was a day, not of the people returning to the land, but of the land returning to the people.

We drove some fifty-five miles through wildly curving mountain roads. *Cerro de Punta,* whose name means hill of the summit, towered four thousand feet high, as we entered the sleepy little village of Jayuya.

112

An *agregado*—a landless farmer—drawing
a lot for twenty acres of land in Jayuya

The landless people stood politely on the veranda of an old
wooden house. Their wives and children and friends spilled over on
the road outside the house. A local official welcomed the visitors.
The first part of the ceremony began.

The Governor held a hat filled with seventy folded slips of paper.
The official called a name. A man stepped forward on the veranda,
put his hand into the hat which the Governor held, and picked a
slip of paper. He opened it and handed it to the official.

"Plot Number 12," the official said loudly so that all the people
on the road could hear.

The Governor shook the man's hand heartily and wished him
well. "Plot Number 12" meant twenty acres of land.

His family, his friends, his landless neighbors applauded.

Another name was called. A quiet, self-effacing man picked a
slip out of the hat. "Plot number 62." The man seemed to tremble.
He brushed his cheek swiftly. He did not see the Governor's hand

outstretched. The Governor understood. He patted the man on the back. The Governor too was silent.

For each man knew that on this morning, his family would begin a new life. The air seemed filled with triumph. The promises that Muñoz and the Popular Democratic Party had made in 1940 and began to fulfill in 1941 were now being carried out in the remotest mountain areas of the island. "We will divide up the land," they had said to the *agregados*. "Huge corporations own the land illegally. Congress set a 500-acre limitation in 1900. But no one enforced the law of the land. We will enforce it. You will own your own home. You will live on your own soil."

The 1940 revolution at the polls had begun as an agrarian reform. The law of the land became the Land Act, the *"Ley de Tierras de Puerto Rico"* of 1941. "The Land of Puerto Rico," it said, "must be considered as a source of life, of dignity and of economic liberty."

The Land Law became the cornerstone of the new government. A census, taken in 1946, revealed that 117,000 families working the land were landless. The Land Authority began to divide up the land in different ways.

Landless families were to be resettled on *agregado* plots, a quarter of an acre to three acres, large enough to raise some vegetables and fruit and have a cow, some pigs and chickens. The program got under way in 1942 and by 1960, over 50,000 *agregado* families had been resettled on land bought by the Commonwealth. Since the average family has eight people, half a million former *agregados* now have a home and a little plot of land. The original plan was to settle 70,000 families in all on these plots. But with migration and some prosperity, the government has lowered the figure to 60,000, and plans to complete this part of the land program by 1963.

The land being subdivided today was another part of the program. It was the "family plan" farm program, called Title VI. Its purpose was to develop lands that could not easily be mechanized, but which could be farmed by a family. These family-size farms called *fincas* ranged from seven to ninety acres; the less productive the soil the larger the farm. Today's land in Jayuya had been divided, under Title VI, into twenty-acre plots. Each of these seventy farmers would have forty years to pay the government back in small monthly payments.

More than 1,000 family-size farms have already been created. The goal is to create 20,000 by 1975. Most of the land was abandoned pasture, bought by the government under amicable terms. The Central Aguirre, a huge sugar mill near Guayama, gave the government 360 acres (selling them for $1.00 to make it legal) to show how much it approved this program. Some private owners were eager to sell; some, of course, fought it. Then the government, under the law, had the right to expropriate the land and make what it considered a reasonable offer for its purchase.

This land in Jayuya was in litigation. For years the *agregados* had worked in the sugar fields with machetes; tractors could not come into these mountains. Some of the land was planted in coffee and fruit. The *agregados* lived on the land in shacks and paid rent to the landowner. A few years ago the landowner shut down most of his sugar operation, sold the sugar mill to a Venezuelan company which shipped all the equipment to Venezuela. The land lay abandoned. The sugar workers were without work. They still had to pay rent, but they had little food and less money.

The government decided to make the land produce again, and give the people work. They offered the owner a price for part of his land. He refused the offer. He could not prevent the government from buying the land, but he could bring an action in court to prove that they had not offered him enough money. That action was now pending, while the government, using its legal authority, was dividing his land. The land would no longer be planted in sugar. These farmers would soon be raising coffee, tobacco, yams, potatoes, and corn for market.

Now came the second part of the day's festivities. The men drew lots for cows.

This was all fun. Around the veranda and on the street, everyone laughed as each cowless farmer picked a number out of the hat, and then went down to the pasture to see what his cow looked like. The numbers weren't rigid. If a man didn't like his cow, he could swap it for another one.

A *campesino* looks over the cow he has just won in the village of Jayuya;
Pablo Vázquez Calcerrada, chief of the Social Programs Administration, and Governor Muñoz Marín are standing to his left

As the morning wore on in the mountainous town, we were ready
for the third part of the ceremony—the inauguration of the $350
houses in a brand new barrio called Comunidad Saliente, about
four miles outside of Jayuya. This was the high point of the day.

For fifteen months these men had worked in teams of five, each
giving one day a week plus a Saturday or Sunday, to build the new
houses.

This was *Ayuda Mutua*—mutual self-help or aided self-help.
Idealistic young men had been sent throughout the island by the
Department of Agriculture to talk to the *agregados,* to explain
mutual self-help. A minimum of seventy-five families would move
out of their scattered shacks into a brand-new community selected
and surveyed by the Department of Agriculture and then approved
by the Planning Board (everything in Puerto Rico is planned!). The
new site would be subdivided into lots for houses, with park areas,

A typical jíbaro house in the hills

schools, a co-operative store, a 4-H Club, a Health Center and a Community Center. Streets would be laid out to follow the slopes and contours of the hills.

Each family which joined the "Aided Self-Help Group" would pay $20 down and $2.50 for charges. For many families in the hills this was a staggering sum of money. But it meant—a house, a real concrete house, free of termites, a home of one's own, a home in which to live and raise children with pride. For the essence of self-help was that the people would help each other in building their own homes.

They received their lots by drawing numbers to make sure that no one was favored. As soon as they had a lot they could begin moving into the community. Some moved their old houses intact,

A team of men working together building a self-help $350 house

pulling them with oxen or a tractor. And now the work of building the houses began.

The Department of Agriculture provided a full-time foreman, the plans for the buildings, and paid for the cement, the cement-mixer, and the truck. The whole house cost the government $350—hence the name $350 houses. The people repaid the cost by paying the Department of Agriculture $2.71 a month rent for ten years. The houses were identical, 18 by 18 feet, with two bedrooms and a living room-dining room on a quarter of an acre of land.

In the months while they were building their houses, the government sent in a team to help educate and orient them—an agronomist to teach them new techniques in farming, a social worker, a health educator, and an engineer.

Putting the final touches to a $350 concrete house;
the former wooden shack home stands next to it

The $350 housing program has caught fire all over the island.
Each year more *campesinos,* more country people, join the self-help
groups. In the beginning fifteen families worked in teams of five.
Now 125 families work together in small teams. Through trial and
error the program has become so efficient that the government now
believes that the more families that work together the better. In late
1959, the ten-thousandth $350 house had been built. 80,000 people
were now living in houses they had built themselves. People from
underdeveloped countries all over the world have come to Puerto
Rico to see if they can adapt the program among their own people.

Traveling along the roads in the evening one often sees an un-
forgettable sight—a human ladder silhouetted against the dark
Caribbean sky. Men are working in conveyor-belt fashion, passing

materials to each other from the men on the ground to the man on the top of the ladder. Long after their working day they are building a row of houses that look, in the twilight, like a row of cakes about to be baked.

The brand-new houses in Comunidad Saliente outside of Jayuya were set in a green valley encircled by three rolling hills in varying shades of green. The houses were painted in bright pinks and greens like the hibiscus which already grew in the front gardens.

The Governor entered the home of a young farm laborer, Luis González Heredia, whose dark hair had been brushed back and who walked with pride through his little home. His eight children followed us quietly, all dressed in party clothes. His wife, red-haired and beaming, wore a maternity dress and stood shyly in the background. One of the daughters, with hair more flaming red than her mother's, with freckles and green eyes, showed us their proudest possession, the refrigerator standing in the place of honor in the living room.

González' family was typical. Nearly every one of the families here had eight children or more. They had worked sporadically for the landowner from whom the government had bought this land, earning less than $281 a year. On the road were some of the shacks which they had moved here to live in, while they built their new houses.

As the celebration began, hundreds of people dressed in their Sunday best assembled in the warm sun while the Governor and the political leaders stood on a palm-thatched platform.

Pablo Vázquez Calcerrada, chief of the Social Programs Administration of the Department of Agriculture, in charge of this whole program, walked to the front of the platform. He looked like an aristocratic Spaniard and talked like a democrat.

"I wish that everyone in Puerto Rico living in a shack would have a house like these houses which you have built yourself. I hope that all of you will be happy in your new homes and keep them always as pretty and clean and well-painted as they are today."

The Vice-President of the House of Representatives, Jorge Font Saldaña called these mutual self-help houses the best example of

A peasant woman receiving the certificate of ownership
for her "aided self-help" $350 house

the co-operation of the Commonwealth with its jíbaros. He talked
of *dignidad*. Now in these new houses each *campesino* could live
and raise his children with *dignidad*.

Three jíbaro musicians sat on the palm-thatched platform playing folk music on native instruments. One played a guitar called a
"cuatro," meaning four, another a *"güiro,"* a hollowed-out gourd
which he scratched with metal prongs, and a third played maracas.
They sang a *"décima,"* a ten-line verse which they had made up
describing this day, telling how the men had built these beautiful
new houses, and thanking the leaders of the government for helping
the jíbaros begin a new life.

Now it was the Governor's turn to speak. "The best speech is these houses," he said.

"Twenty years ago, we were the same people. But we lived hopelessly. Now we have hope. We live together as a family. We are many people joined together. We are the family of Puerto Rico."

His hands were never still. He kept touching his heart, then moving his hands toward the people. His hands told them eloquently that he was talking from his heart to them. He kept repeating the word "family," *la familia de Puerto Rico.*

"What the family of Puerto Rico has done here today is the story of our whole island. The tempo of the last twenty years has made a transformation in the land. We have had many problems. We have had grave difficulties. We have made mistakes and we have many faults. But we are building a good civilization. The change which has come in the last twenty years is the greatest I know in the entire history of my people."

The jíbaros in their Sunday shirts and straw hats nodded.

The face of the jíbaro is truly the face of Puerto Rico—the man with the *pava,* the large straw hat, waving his machete, cutting his way through the tall, soft jungle of sugar cane. Now he was listening to his Governor describe, with Spanish eloquence, this rare thing that the family of Puerto Rico had done for itself.

Muñoz began to call each name, and each *campesino* came forward. Muñoz leaned out of the thatched platform and handed each one his certificate of ownership. Each man grasped Muñoz' outstretched hand.

The musicians played a Puerto Rican song that had rarely had more meaning than it did this bright Sunday morning. "Now I have my house."

Around the island, eighty thousand people now living in their own $350 houses could sing, "Now I have my house."

"Owning your own home, after having been a squatter, has a great emotional impact," Luis Rivera Santos, the forty-six-year-old Secretary of Agriculture and Commerce, told me a few days later when we discussed the festival in Jayuya. The Secretary was one of the "founding fathers" of the $350 houses. He had in fact been Executive Director of the Social Programs Administration from

1949 until 1955, when he became Secretary of the whole department.

"In twenty years," he said, *"agregados* have been moved into village settlements. In these twenty years, we have remade a way of agrarian life. I think it is the first time in history that this was done."

The most spectacular agrarian reform in the peaceful revolution was not in farming but in housing. It was an agrarian reform in the human terms of bettering the lives of the farmers, not yet in the concrete terms of bettering the techniques of farming. In a country that had been neglected for over four hundred years, it was perhaps inevitable that the first steps of the reform would be human rather than technological.

The Secretary of Agriculture talked with pride of the meaning of this Puerto Rican agrarian revolution. "It was not only that in the villages we could provide the *campesinos* with services at reasonable costs which we couldn't do when they lived scattered over the hills. The important thing was that the families developed a sense of responsibility in solving their own problems. This spirit of self-help has generated a lot of power. It influences our whole way of life. It has tremendous influence for the future of Puerto Rico, and perhaps for the whole world."

Farm experts have questioned whether the island can ever feed itself, even if it were farmed better than it is today. Actually few countries in the world truly feed themselves; they import from each other. Even the United States, rich in food, imports some of its mainstays like coffee and bananas. Each year Puerto Rico exports to the United States some $125,000,000 worth of food—of sugar, pineapple, citrus fruits, molasses. It imports, among other things, about $30,000,000 worth of rice, $25,000,000 worth of meat, $8,000,000 worth of lard, and $12,000,000 worth of dried milk.

Certainly, as it improves its farm techniques, it will probably need to import less food. Already it produces remarkably sweet pineapples, bananas of all shapes and sizes, grapefruits, mangoes, limes, oranges, and avocados. Acerola berries, grown easily, have more vitamin C than oranges. Still the island imports more than 60% of the food it eats. The more the population explodes, the less likely it is that the island can feed itself.

"Our challenge," the Secretary of Agriculture and Commerce told me, "is that we have a high density of population—about 650 people per square mile. Even though we are doing better than many countries with soil like ours, we should be doing better than we are."

It is possible that Fomento was able to make giant strides in Puerto Rico just because there had been no industry. Agriculture is the victim of four hundred and fifty years of farming. It is hard to change old patterns and generations of defeat.

As industry grows on the island, agriculture suffers the same problems it faces in the States—farm workers leave the rural areas to take jobs in the new plants. The level of salaries in the plants is higher than on the land. The farmers themselves making the transition from the land to industries move into towns which are unable to house them. So they swell the slums at the edge of the towns.

To keep the people on the land, the Department of Agriculture has begun ambitious programs. Its goal is to raise the level of living to $2,000 per family in 1975. This would be the highest per capita income in Latin America.

It has programs for increasing milk production and developing livestock all over the island. It has largely eradicated cattle diseases such as tuberculosis and brucellosis, and is rapidly eradicating ticks. It is cross-breeding native Puerto Rican cows which gave little milk with Black Angus for beef and with Holsteins for dairy. Pasteurized milk is now sold not only in the cities but in the little *colmados,* the country stores in the hills.

Sugar cane continues to be the island's major crop, livestock its second, coffee its third, and tobacco its fourth. The government is now sending coffee farmers to Latin America and livestock and truck farmers to the States to learn new farm practices.

In 1897 Puerto Rico produced 70,000 tons of sugar; by 1934 it had produced about 1,000,000 tons; by 1959 only 1,100,000 tons. Now the sugar growers are trying to raise more sugar on less land.

In the depressed thirties, Puerto Rico was a typical one-crop economy. In 1935 sugar employed about 100,000 workers, over 20% of all the island's wage earners. But they worked only five months a year and starved the rest of the year. A report made by

Laborers in a pineapple field at harvest time

the Brookings Institution in Washington in 1929 revealed that the average Puerto Rican field worker was earning approximately twelve cents a day.

In 1934, sugar workers already oppressed, hopelessly under-nourished and diseased, were struck an almost fatal blow. The United States passed the Costigan-Jones Act which set up a quota system for sugar production. Plantations were paid *not* to grow sugar. Thousands of workers were deprived even of their twelve cents a day.

The rich grew richer and the poor grew poorer. Four large sugar

Jíbaros harvesting sugar cane with machetes

plantations, called *centrales,* the Fajardo Sugar, the Eastern Puerto Rican Sugar, the Central Aguirre, and the South Puerto Rico, with local capital and absentee capital from the States and Europe, produced most of the sugar on the island. The small independent Puerto Rican planters, called *colonos,* grew sugar on their own or rented land and then generally sold it to the large *centrales* to be pressed and processed.

World War II brought a new demand, and sugar became king again in Puerto Rico. Under the 500-acre Law, the government began to break up some of the huge corporate sugar holdings. It helped the farmers set up proportional-profit farms where the workers received minimum wages established by law, plus bonuses on profits. The government takes no profit from the farms, but a certain amount is deducted for repayment of capital investment. The government also bought mills and set up co-operatives to run them, such as the *Central Lafayette* and the *Central Los Caños* near Arecibo.

One spring during the sugar harvest, when the island seemed covered with tall waving fields of cane, I visited *Los Caños*. For miles around the *central,* the jíbaros walked through the tall fields cutting the cane with machetes and loading it on trucks. We followed the trucks as they drove on to the grounds of the huge mill. Cranes lifted the stalks of sugar cane into the refinery where, in half an hour, giant machines pressed and ground each truckload of cane into bulk sugar. Mountains of sugar waited to be loaded again on trucks to be taken to the sugar ships bound for the States. Three hundred men were employed working on eight-hour shifts twenty-four hours a day four months a year.

On May 15, 1948, Puerto Rico passed the first unemployment compensation law enacted for any agricultural workers in any of the territories of the United States or the mainland. The law was idealistic; but the benefits were a pittance. The unemployed sugar workers received about $3 a week for a maximum of $27 for the "dead time."

The government recognized, of course, that no family could live on such compensation. But it was a beginning. Now the government has established a system of compensation for those who lost their employment because of the bulk shipment of sugar, and is working on compensation for workers displaced by mechanization.

The "dead time" in the sugar industry still plagues the island. It explains part of the present migration to the States; more and more of the people leaving Puerto Rico come directly from the rural areas. It also explains the migration inside the island, as farm workers migrate to the cities in search of work.

Many, who do not want to leave the island for good, go to the States for a few months each year on the migrant agricultural program. But for those who stay on the island during the dead time, there is genuine hardship.

They may get a few dollars in compensation and surplus federal foods. But their real social security is inside the family. No jíbaro

A sugar refinery

lets another jíbaro starve. Those who have a little extra food or money share it with their less fortunate relatives.

"Do you know what Puerto Rican social security is?" R. E. García Bottari, the thirty-two-year-old dean of students of the University of Puerto Rico at Mayagüez told me one day as we were walking in the rain through the beautiful campus of the College of Agriculture and Mechanic Arts. Without waiting for an answer, he smiled and said, "A man may be living in a one-room shack with his wife and eight children. His neighbor dies. There are three children left without a father. This man is their godfather. He takes them to live at his house with his eight children. This is Puerto Rican social security."

Everyone who travels through the hills discovers this for himself. Where three are eating, five can eat. This has helped keep the Puerto Rican jíbaro alive. They are a people full of traditions, the greatest of which is their hospitality. The jíbaro living in the humblest house in the hills will invite you in. Just as among the Eskimos in Alaska, you dare not tell a jíbaro in his house that you like something. Immediately he hands it to you eagerly. "Take it. It is yours."

It is this quality that has endeared the Puerto Ricans to many of the mainlanders who have established permanent roots on the island.

Dr. Harry E. Warmke, Director of the Federal Experiment Station of the United States Department of Agriculture in Mayagüez, who has been in Puerto Rico over fourteen years, told me as we sat with his wife and their five-year-old daughter Julie in his quiet home on the station, "I'd rather live in Puerto Rico than in Washington, D. C. or in my wife's native state, Maine. It's this wonderful hospitality. It's their willingness to accept outsiders, their warmth. It's the attitude of the common man.

"I remember when we first came to Puerto Rico, we drove up the mountains near Añasco on the coast north of Mayagüez. We got out of the car and walked. There was no road at all. The people were walking over the mountains covered with growing mountain rice. We stood admiring the rice.

"They said, 'Take it. It's much better than you can buy in the store.' They had worked so hard getting it. Yet they gave us a big bagful. They would have been insulted if we hadn't taken it. Someone gave us three eggs. One man wanted us to be sure to go to the top of the mountain.

" 'From the hills of Puerto Rico,' he said, 'you can see the whole world.' "

CHAPTER 9

The People Go to School

Education is bursting out over the island. Education has become its lifeblood. Everyone wants schooling for his children, his family, himself. One third of Puerto Rico's entire population in the hills and in the cities goes to school.

The statistics on literacy tell a thrilling story—in sixty years, the United States has helped the island people carry through the American dream of public school education.

In 1898, less than 20% of the people could read and write. Out of some 260,600 school-age children, barely 25,600 went to school. Like most of Spain's colonies, the island had widespread illiteracy. Today there is 86% literacy, and of the island's children within the age brackets of six to eighteen, 85% now go to school.

It is upon education that Governor Muñoz is now focusing the full power of government thinking. "We're going to make great changes in our whole educational system," he told me one day in the spring of 1958. With Doña Inés, who had been a teacher, we were watching the mist settle over the island's mountains from the terrace at Jájome Alto. As twilight fell, the lights disappeared one by one on the Caribbean coast south of the mountains.

"I've been here nearly a week just reading and thinking about education," he said. "I'm concerned and disturbed about education,

Children in the nursery and day-care center of the Luis Llorens
Torres housing project in San Juan learning English songs

just as you are in the States. We've got to rethink our whole approach, and start making changes."

Two years later, the Governor had crystallized some of his thinking. He opened his Annual Message to the Third Legislative Assembly in San Juan on January 19, 1960, with a discussion of education.

"We are now starting a new decade," he said. "I propose that we devote special attention to what kind of civilization, what kind of culture, what deep and good manner of living do the people of Puerto Rico want to make for themselves on the basis of their increasing economic prosperity.

"This is the true ideal of a people, their real finality. . . . If a good civilization is the final goal . . . we must set above all others the duty of education.

"Let us start by raising the teacher to the position of prestige that is proper to his task. Let us make the resolution that . . . education in Puerto Rico, in all its aspects, shall have reached a level comparable with that of the states and countries best served by education. Teachers' compensation is an integral part of the great reform. Let us also determine—beginning right now!—to have that part of the recognition we owe to the teacher reach before the end of the decade at least the levels obtaining in the United States.

"Whether the kind of education being given to children and young people is adequate for a free world, is something that is being questioned not only in Puerto Rico but also in the United States and many other parts of the world," the Governor continued. "Public schools have discharged in Puerto Rico a highly commendable function, deepening our devotion to a democratic way of life and our respect for the dignity of man. They have performed their task during a period of sixty years amid great difficulties, for until a few years ago they functioned under a highly centralized, colonial system, with appointments of the commissioners of education not originating in Puerto Rico."

In 1959, education was so important that $62,000,000, nearly one third of the total budget of $200,000,000, was for schools. For the year 1960–61, the Governor recommended appropriating $88,000,000, with $12,700,000 for increases in teachers' salaries. Good education hinged on good teachers. It was a basic truth that every Board of Education on the mainland had learned.

It has been said that when Spain came to a territory she built a church; when the United States came she built a school. The tradition has continued. Now new modern schools are being built in the towns and the hills. Some of the schools in San Juan today are a modern architect's dream, with bright painted walls, colonnaded corridors, and sunlit rooms. The students too, boys in summer shirts and girls in uniforms of white blouses and bright-colored jumpers, look spotless. It is hard to tell which youngsters come from good housing and which ones come from the wooden shacks of the slums.

The parents, not the school, decide whether their daughters should wear uniforms; they choose the material, color, and style.

A class in the new Albert Einstein Junior and Senior High School, San Juan. The girls wear turquoise-and-white school uniforms

Not all schools have uniforms, but those that do, have colors ranging from soft pastels to warm maroon and royal blue. The girls in the new Albert Einstein Junior and Senior High School in San Juan wear a lovely turquoise to match the aqua color of their exciting new school building.

"We are trying to rear a well-fed, well-dressed, oriented and democratic generation," the Secretary of Education, Efraín Sánchez Hidalgo, told me one day in his office in Hato Rey in San Juan. He is a forty-one-year-old Puerto Rican who received his Ph.D. at Columbia University, taught education at the University of Puerto Rico, and was appointed Secretary of Education in 1957. "There is a new spirit here," he told me. "Before this everyone was lamenting. Everyone was saying, '*Ay bendito*' (literally, "oh, the blessed one" —colloquially, "oh me, oh my!"). It was our lament. Now there is a spirit of hope. I come from the rural zone of Moca, near Aguadilla. I had to walk twelve kilometers every day to go to school.

I had to take off my shoes and socks, and when I got to school I had to wash my feet. Now there is a road there, electricity, television, aqueducts. The barefoot jíbaro of my day is disappearing. And the public schools are helping him to disappear.

"Nearly all the officials of Puerto Rico have come from the public schools. The schools have been a seed-bed of public administration. That is why the people have faith in the officials."

Representatives of the underdeveloped countries who come to Puerto Rico are fascinated by the history of public education on the island. To people who come from Jordan or Egypt or Ghana or Liberia, Puerto Rico's school system seems more advanced, more progressive, better able to cope with the needs of a society changing swiftly from agriculture to industry than most of these visitors hope to see in their countries in the next two generations.

"The Puerto Rican Department of Education," Dr. Harold Fields, member of the Board of Examiners of the Board of Education of the City of New York, told me, "is doing the most outstanding job in the Caribbean. It is setting an example for the people of all the islands in the Caribbean and all the countries that border it. The Puerto Ricans are entitled to great credit and I think we should give it to them."

In a report which Dr. Fields wrote in November 1955 as educational consultant to the Commonwealth, he summarized public school education on the island as "a pattern of education that couples realism with imagination."

Yet in the dynamics of the revolution in Puerto Rico, even with a government eager to support changes in progress, education has not been able to make the rapid strides made in industry. To be sure, the public school system, compared with most countries in Latin America or the Arab world, is a model of progressivism. But it is not enough to take pride in being "ahead" of Egypt or Jordan. Public education in Puerto Rico still lags behind the needs of its people.

Part of Puerto Rico's school problem is its exploding population. This is a country of young people and young child-bearers. In the United States 33% of the population is under 19 years of age; in Puerto Rico 55% of the population is under 19. Each year the

Dr. Harold Fields, member of the Board of Examiners of New York
City's Board of Education, observing a third-grade class
of the Rosa María Arcay School, Cataño

number of children who enter schools increases. Each year "the
eagerness for education" strains an already overtaxed system. But
the ideal of free public education continues to be the focal point
around which the revolution revolves.

Puerto Rico suffers from two enormous shortages—shortages of
schoolrooms and shortages of teachers. New schools go up all the
time, but the need is so great that in some towns I saw classes meeting in empty stores. In many schools the smallest register of any
teacher is 81; the largest in one school is 104. Half the children
come in the morning, half in the afternoon.

Even in the brand new Albert Einstein High School with 1,650 pupils, there is already so much overcrowding that no student can go to school all day. The eleventh and twelfth graders have classes from 7:30 in the morning to 12:30. The others study from 12:30 to 5:30.

Yet on the whole there is such a real desire to go to school and such genuine affection between pupils and teachers, that you often see morning students standing around a school building in the afternoon, peering through the windows with hunger not for food but for learning.

Puerto Rico's army of teachers, 14,000 strong, are among the most respected members of society. But they are scarcely half the army the island needs if it is to give its children proper schooling. One of the reasons for the shortage, as the Governor pointed out in his Annual Message, is low salaries. A teacher with a Normal School diploma is paid as little as $150 a month. Yet the basic training is good. Teachers receive a two-year training program at the University of Puerto Rico, where they are given not only college courses but an introduction to the philosophy and techniques of education.

It is typical of the responsibility which the Government of Puerto Rico bears for its entire citizenry, that it sends good teachers to the remote hills. Beginning teachers are assigned where there are vacancies, in urban or rural schools. Their coming is a blessing for the people in the hills.

The discipline in every school I visited was remarkable. There was no tension. The teachers spoke softly. The atmosphere was relaxed. The quiet absorption seemed to come from within the pupils themselves, in their newly born passion for learning.

The costs of education to Puerto Rico are staggering. The Federal Government in Washington makes a contribution to the Puerto Rican schools in vocational education, in free lunches, and in the teaching of science. But the Commonwealth schools provide not only teachers and all the books which are given free from the first grade through the eighth grade; they also provide free shoes to every child who needs them, free transportation, scholarships for the mentally gifted, a weekly newspaper for the parents called

Bomberitos—"Little Firemen"—schoolchildren of Utuado
parading to teach their community fire prevention

Semana, with a circulation of a quarter of a million, a monthly newspaper for teachers called *Educación,* and a weekly paper called *Escuela,* published in separate editions for elementary school and senior high school students.

The great controversy in Puerto Rico's educational system has been the teaching of English. There was no problem when Spain owned the island. Spanish was the language taught to the privileged few who attended school. When the Americans came, they found so few teachers that they had to bring qualified people from the States to teach in the rapidly opening schools. The schools became completely English-speaking because the teachers spoke no Spanish.

To many Puerto Ricans it seemed absurd to have their Spanish-

speaking children learn all their lessons in English. The cruel jest
one heard was that "the people are illiterate in two languages."

The debate raged for decades. From a pedagogical problem, it
became a political one. Even policy-making educators became
more interested in making headlines than in making headway.
When Puerto Rico became practically autonomous with the Elective Governor Act in 1947, the school system was completely
revised. Everything was taught in Spanish; English was taught as a
foreign language for fifty minutes every day.

Still the debate continued. Some of the *Estadistas* clamored for
a return to English as the language of the schools. The *Independentistas* denounced the move as "cultural imperialism." Pupils
were confused. Parents were confused. The Spanish-English controversy became a political tug-of-war.

Certainly English is better and more widely spoken on the island
today than it was a few years ago, but everyone admits there is
room for vast improvement. There has been an exchange of teachers
with the States, but the program has been slow and not very successful. Groups of Puerto Rican teachers have been sent to colleges
on the mainland to live in an English-speaking environment. But the
numbers sent were few, and it was soon obvious that they talked
English in their classes but reverted to Spanish as soon as they
were together in their dormitories. The average English teacher on
the island speaks with a marked Spanish accent, which the students
inevitably imitate. The new goal is bilingualism, but, as one educator told me, "Bilingualism doesn't mean 90% of one language and
10% of another." The country is working toward a new middle-of-
the-road solution.

In the little island of Vieques, part of Puerto Rico, off its eastern
coast, I discovered that many of the schoolchildren spoke English
quite well. The American Marines were based on the island, and
the Department of Education enlisted them and especially their
wives in helping the schools teach English. To be sure, Vieques
has English background and ancestry. Its early settlers were
English and French, not Spanish.

Although public education for all people has been the island's
great goal, one of the ironies today is that most of the middle and

Ponce High School

wealthy classes do not send their children to the public schools. Many of them told me that the classes were too crowded; there were split sessions; and, in their opinion, not enough English was taught. Thus the public schools of Puerto Rico suffer because they lack the advantage of economic and cultural integration.

Private schools are all over the island. The Catholic Church is trying to win back churchgoers through its parochial schools. Nuns, with a good deal of teaching experience, are brought from the States to teach. Their schools are not free. Even in elementary school the cost of tuition, uniforms, books, and "co-operation" is about $250 a year. But in the parochial schools there are no split or interlocking sessions; the pupils have a full school day.

The Protestants, too, are building parochial schools on the island. In Metropolitan San Juan alone, there are five Protestant schools with English as their language of instruction; eight Protestant schools use both Spanish and English; and eleven nonsectarian schools use both languages. Of the better-known English-speaking schools, Robinson School in San Juan receives a subsidy from Methodist women in the States. The Episcopalians have built St. John School. And there are two nonsectarian schools which

were set up with the help of Fomento for the children of the mainlanders, Commonwealth School and San Juan School.

Puerto Rico has broadly modeled its schools upon the schools in
the mainland with the 6-3-3 plan; six years of elementary school,
three years of junior high, and three years of senior high school.
But the island has also worked out phases of education born of its
special needs.

To make the swift change into the twentieth century, Puerto Rico
has built the Miguel Such Technical School in Hato Rey in San
Juan. Here the students learn more than fifty trades. They are
taught, among others things, to be toolmakers, carpenters, elec-
tricians, radio and television technicians, auto and airplane mechanics. There are even fully equipped beauty parlors and barber
shops in which the students are trained. There are four vocational
high schools on the island and eleven comprehensive schools offering academic, commercial, vocational, and industrial courses. Today
some seven thousand teen-age boys and girls in the vocational high
schools are preparing themselves for a productive life on the island
or on the mainland if they migrate.

The rural schools too are trying to teach their students how to
live in the new Puerto Rico. The Second-Unit Rural Schools are
regular junior high schools that offer vocational courses in home
economics, native crafts, agriculture, and industrial arts. Some of
the schools have animal husbandry programs, and the boys are
encouraged to get good cattle from government agencies to improve
their stock.

The girls learn cooking, baking, canning, dressmaking, hygiene,
and nutrition to help change the rice-and-beans diet of the *campesinos*. Each rural and city school has a federally sponsored free
School Lunch Program with carefully planned hot meals, made up
of surplus canned foods sent by the Federal Government, and sup-
plemented by meats, locally grown vegetables, and milk. For some
children in the cities and in the hills, this is the only adequate meal
of the day.

Teen-agers in the hills of Puerto Rico, like teen-agers on the
plains of Kansas, join the 4-H Clubs, the Boy Scouts, Girl Scouts,
the Future Homemakers of America, the Future Farmers of Amer-

A veteran of World War II who is a student in the vocational
agriculture class at Sabana Seca Second-Unit Rural School

ica, and exchange visits with each other. During a recent Christmas
vacation, seven teen-age schoolboys of Italian parents, living in
New York's East Harlem, were brought by the Office of the
Commonwealth to Puerto Rico to live among Puerto Ricans of
their own age.

Under the guidance of a former professor of the Yale University
School of Drama, Leopoldo Santiago Lavandero, the Department
of Education has set up all-day educational television and radio

programs. Station WIPR, in a new $2,000,000 building, has audio-visual classes for adults, for home-bound children, for cardiacs and spastics, and for healthy children who, because of the over-crowding, attend school only half a day.

Education is free, but for many Puerto Rican families, even free education is a luxury. The little boy whom you see in the school-room during the morning learning to read and write may be the boy shining shoes in the evening in front of your hotel.

A few years ago it would have been unthinkable for a boy or girl from a "nice" family to work his way through college. Today. with the Americanization of Puerto Rico, Dean R. E. García, dean of students of the University of Puerto Rico at Mayagüez, told me, a great number of college students are helping their professors, working as laboratory assistants, working on construction jobs, holding part-time jobs in the supermarkets and department stores, especially during the Christmas rush and on Mother's Day—one of the biggest shopping days in Puerto Rico, when every woman in the family gets a present.

Intellectual life on the island is centered around the campus of the University of Puerto Rico. Founded in 1903, it has grown steadily until today there are 16,923 students. It is really no longer a single university, but a university system with three campuses. The main campus is at Río Piedras, on the outskirts of San Juan, where courses are given in the humanities, social science, natural science, education, law, pharmacy, business administration, social work, and public administration. The various health units—the School of Medicine and Tropical Medicine and the Dental School —are in old San Juan. The campus at Mayagüez on the west coast has the College of Agriculture and Mechanic Arts (called A. and M.) and its own school of arts and sciences. The University gives M.A. degrees, but no Ph.D.'s.

There are actually four universities and a college in this little island, the University of Puerto Rico in San Juan and Mayagüez; the Catholic University in Ponce administered by the Church; the Inter-American University, a Protestant University, in San Germán; and the Sacred Heart College in San Juan. The University of Puerto Rico is government-supported, its budget fixed by the

Main building, University of Puerto Rico, at Río Piedras

Commonwealth. There are a great many scholarships and tuition is $72 per semester.

Any student from the mainland and from any country in the world may enter, provided he has a high school diploma and passes the entrance examinations. Courses are taught in both English and Spanish since the university is completely bilingual. There are Puerto Rican professors who teach in English and North American professors who teach in Spanish. Dean R. E. García told me, "People from the States are astonished at what a role education plays in Puerto Rico. I talked recently to the deans of all the colleges, meeting at Harvard. They were amazed at all the things going on in Puerto Rico, in agriculture, in engineering, in science. We have a laboratory for hydraulics and another laboratory for thermodynamics. We're building a nuclear reactor right here on our campus. Fomento has an office right in the University so that graduates can go right from here into industry."

In Río Piedras, Jaime (pronounced Hymay) Benítez is the Chancellor of all the campuses of the University. When Benítez speaks to the students, he talks their language, full of the colloquialisms and slang of Puerto Rico. The University is his life. He lives on the campus in a comfortable modern home a few minutes' walk from his office in the tall tower building which is the landmark of the University.

A small, thin, tense, and intense man in his early fifties, who somehow made me think of a Spanish toreador, Benítez slumped back in his heavy, dark-stained wooden chair behind a huge, dark desk cluttered with papers. We talked of the social revolution in Puerto Rico, a revolution in which Benítez, then barely thirty, had been a leader in the inner circle. It was in the University that he saw the clearest proof of social change.

"This," he said, "is the real center of vitality, of hopefulness, of young men and women throbbing with eagerness, with enthusiasm, with vision of a healthier and more joyful life.

"Education is available to all, it opens the door for the social transcending of caste and class status. The sons and daughters of the unemployed, of the peddlers, of the bus boys and the seamstresses, of the sugar cane workers and the jíbaros, of parents who had never gone to school—through their university degree they become leaders in their society. Each year we graduate close to 3,000 students who are absorbed immediately into the ranks of professors, teachers, agronomists, engineers, public administrators, doctors, lawyers.

"This is the ideological center of the revolution. The beauty of the situation is that all this has happened without the shedding of blood."

CHAPTER 10

Mores, Morals and "Mitas"

Puerto Rico is a relaxed island. Relaxation is a philosophy of life.
This is no siesta-land. The Puerto Rican is not the cartoon Latin
American, with a sombrero pulled over his eyes, sleeping lazily
in the midday sun. He works hard, but he relaxes gracefully.

The stereotype of the Puerto Ricans in the crumbling brownstones of New York dissolves completely as you travel around the
island. There is a soft-spoken graciousness, a quiet dignity that
you find in nearly everyone from the poorest peasant in the hills to
the wealthiest sugar cane owner in Ponce or the busiest government
official in teeming San Juan.

What Puerto Ricans have, that few mainlanders are aware of, is
a *"sentido de dignidad."* It is more than the sense of dignity that the
Spanish words imply. It is *"consideración y respeto."* It is an appre-
ciation of the human being as a whole man.

This is a relaxed land, and even the prisons are relaxed.

Prisoners can leave the prison walls every day to work in *Ayuda
Mutua,* in the mutual self-help houses. In the El Embalse project
of the Urban Renewal Housing Corporation in San Juan, I watched
five prisoners building homes for a blind man and for five widows
who had no male relatives to build for them. The families paid the
prisoners twenty-five cents a day and gave them lunch.

Life is relaxed inside the prison gates too. Every three months, prisoners who are not repeaters of felony crimes, are allowed to go home to their wives and families for fifty-two hours. The chief of the Penal Institutions Division of the Justice Department, Porfirio Díaz Santana, told me, "The law authorizes these furloughs for selected inmates. In only one or two instances have they failed to come back. One got drunk, and he didn't dare to come back. The other one showed up one day late."

In the huge white concrete prison in Río Piedras, I walked through the carpentry shops where teachers from the Department of Education were training the prisoners. They were busy making tables, desks, and chairs for the public schools, earning from 25¢ to $1.25 a day. At four o'clock they were to stop work in the shops and re-enter the prison gates. They sat leisurely on the ground, waiting for the gong to sound four o'clock. It was hard to believe this was a prison. There were two or three guards, who carried neither guns nor nightsticks.

"It's too dangerous for the guards," the kindly deputy warden told me. "The prisoners might try to disarm them; somebody could get hurt."

Relaxation is a profound thing too. In this land where people's skins range from white to copper to mulatto and black, there is no color line. The Speaker of the House of Representatives is Ramos Antonini, a Negro.

There is, to be sure, some prejudice among some of the people. But it is rarely brought into the open. The government's policy is to protect its Negro Puerto Ricans from the whip-lash of discrimination.

Recently some farmers in our southern states tried to sign contracts with Puerto Ricans for seasonal work. The Government of Puerto Rico politely refused. Its policy, it explained, is to send seasonal workers only to communities which guarantee by law that there will be no discrimination.

Washington was bewildered. A federal official was dispatched to the island to discover why the Commonwealth itself was practicing discrimination. The Puerto Rican Government explained carefully that most Puerto Ricans were not conscious of a color barrier.

Plaza at Guayama

Innocently, in the South, they could get into trouble. They could not send Puerto Ricans to any states that practiced discrimination by law.

The people have a gentle romantic love for their whole island, but they are fiercely and passionately patriotic about their home town.

Theirs is a nationalism, not for Puerto Rico, but for the towns in which they live. Ponceños tell you that the only city in the island to live in, because of its Spanish beauty and tradition, is Ponce. The Mayagüezanos tell you that you do not know Puerto Rico unless you have lived in Mayagüez and smelled the fresh sweet smell of the mango trees. It rains almost every single afternoon in Mayagüez and the people say they love it.

"I wouldn't live in Ponce, if they gave it to me," a Mayagüezano told me one day when we were caught in the sudden downpour. "It's too dry there all the time. This air! Ah! It's what makes the city so green and the girls so pretty."

Everyone knows that San Juan is not Puerto Rico, yet it could be hard to convince a Sanjuanero. To him San Juan is all that counts in Puerto Rico just as to a jíbaro, New York is the United States.

The nationalism of the towns is fiercest in sporting events. The country is baseball- and basketball-happy, and each town has its home team. Caguas on the mountain road from San Juan to Ponce is known to be such a poor loser that people travel specially to Caguas not so much to see two teams play, as to see a whole town bait the umpire or get into fist fights. Some of the people of Caguas are known to make vows to the Holy Virgin to walk on their knees to San Juan, twenty-two miles away, if their team wins.

The names of the basketball teams in each town are famous throughout the island. In Ponce they are the *Leones*—Lions. In Arecibo they are the *Capitanes*—the Captains. In San Juan they are ironically *Los Santos*—the Saints. In San Germán they are *Potritos*—the Ponies. The Ponies are supposed to be young men but many of them have grown old in the field. There are doctors and lawyers who play on the teams. They are all amateurs with the passion of amateurs. When the Ponies drive off to another town to play, nuns go up in the hills and pray for them.

There are people who say that hurricanes are born in Puerto Rico, but no good Puerto Rican believes that. The theory is that hurricanes are manufactured mainly in the South Atlantic and the Caribbean, as the hot winds from the equator meet the cool easterly trade winds of the islands.

One night in August 1959, warnings were issued all over the island. Hurricane Edith was about to hit. Rain pounded the island. The hotels and department stores nailed planks of wood across their windows. The banks were boarded up. People pulled in their terrace furniture, rushed to the stores, and in panic bought stocks of canned food, candles and flashlights, batteries, hurricane lamps, kerosene stoves. There was real fear in many hearts that night—fear not only for themselves and their homes, but for the terrible destruction that might hit the farms and industries of the island and cost millions of dollars.

Yet despite the fear, most people were joking. One man coming out of a supermarket, his arms loaded with bundles, said, "Don't worry. No hurricane with an American name ever hits Puerto Rico." A man waiting for a bus on Ponce de León Avenue said, "There can't be any real danger. My callouses don't hurt." Every radio bulletin carried the comforting superstition of the jíbaros. "This has been a bad year for avocados. There has never been a hurricane on the island when the avocado season is a poor one."

Some of the more pleasure-loving people, with the psychology of a soldier's last fling, decided to eat, drink, and be merry before Edith struck. Some prayed, some sang, some danced, some made jokes, some argued, some fought, some stole, some sat remembering all the superstitions their grandmothers had learned from their grandmothers, but most stayed awake waiting for the hurricane to lift off their roofs, bend the coconut palms, and completely destroy the shacks in El Fanguito and La Perla.

But Edith blew her top at sea. The next morning the sun shone soft and warm on the island. The hotels put their beach umbrellas around the swimming pools. The banks and department stores unboarded their windows. The housewives hung their wash out in the yards. Food bought in panic had to be eaten in haste. Families that had closed their own rather flimsy houses and gone to stay with neighbors returned home. San Juan went back to its usual hectic, horn-honking traffic jam and the rest of the island settled back with relief.

This is a relaxed land, and even morals are relaxed. Almost everyone accepts a double standard, and every class has people who practice it.

The double standard has its roots in history. Four hundred years ago, this was an island of men without women, of *conquistadores* and buccaneers who took native women as they found them and gave them sons and daughters in a casual intermingling of Indian, African, and European blood.

Illegitimacy has been legally outlawed. One of the first laws enacted by the Popular Democratic Party declared that every child was legitimate. At birth every child is registered with a father's and a mother's name. One of the axioms on the island is *"No hay hijo sin padre,"*—"there is no son without a father."

Life in a one-room shack, in the slums or in the hills, certainly contributes to early sex knowledge. When seven or eight children sleep in the same shack with parents, aunts, uncles, godfathers, or boarders, a knowledge of the facts of life seems almost built-in.

Yet despite the double standard, the family is the basis of life in Puerto Rico. It is the family that exercises social control. Rich or poor, married in a church or by mutual consent, the father is the head of the household. He may even be the head of two or three households.

Girls are expected to be virgins when they marry; boys would be ridiculed if they were. Divorce is, of course, not permitted in the Catholic Church, but divorces are unnecessary if there has been no marriage. In some of the smaller towns, I was told of people who wanted to be married in the church. Each time they decided to marry a different partner, they went to a different church. Others who want to be faithful to one woman cannot afford the two-dollar license and the whole ceremony of posting banns and having a wedding party.

Unquestionably the greatest change in family life has come through Fomento. In the forties, a number of anthropologists predicted ruin and doom for Puerto Rico's native culture and the simple primitive happiness of its people through the onslaught of technology. The people of Puerto Rico may very well have been happier before the industrial revolution changed their lives in the forties; but they also died faster, were hungry longer, and had more disease.

The Americanization of Puerto Rico, which began in a desultory way in 1898 and became full-fledged when the United States Army moved into Puerto Rico in 1940 at the outbreak of World War II, has struck hard blows against many of the old Spanish traditions.

Patio near the *Ayuntamiento*, the seventeenth-century City Hall in Old San Juan

"We live by Spanish traditions," is still a phrase of pride, though everyone is aware that many of the traditions may be gone by the next generation or sooner. Meanwhile some of them hang on, especially the chaperones and the coming-out parties of the upper- and middle-income families.

One Saturday night at the exclusive Casino de Puerto Rico in San Juan, thirty girls made their debut in exquisite white gowns, each of which cost about $1,000. The girls were slim, tiny-waisted, with red, blonde, or shining black curls framing their faces. Each mother, nervous and tense, hovered over her daughter, fixing a stray hair, powdering a nose, or pulling a huge ribbon or cabbage flower on the back of the gown.

It was hard to believe these beautiful young women were only fifteen. "Our girls mature very young here," Mrs. Mariano Ramírez, whose lawyer-husband was vice-president of the Casino de Puerto Rico, told me. "I think it's not only the climate. It's because they are always with their mothers or older people who chaperone them. Their mothers go with them to every dance and every party until they are twenty-one. If the mother cannot go then she sends an aunt or a godmother (a very important figure in Puerto Rico) or some woman relative. People talk a great deal in our towns, and no boy would take a girl out who isn't chaperoned, unless she is 'that kind of girl.' "

Even in religion, Puerto Rico is a relaxed island. It is a Catholic country; but the Catholic Church is quite different from the Catholic Church in the States or in Ireland. It is a relaxed, easy-going Mediterranean Church. This is a Catholic country but there are government birth-control stations and a divorced man is Governor.

The Catholic Church suffered a loss of prestige under the Spanish occupation. As Spanish rule was coming to an end toward the close of the nineteenth century, Puerto Rico began to strive for greater religious, political, and economic freedom. The first Protestant churches appeared in Ponce and Vieques while the Spaniards still owned the island. When the Americans came in 1898, Protestant missionaries were suddenly free to come too. But even while they successfully proselytized sections of the population, Catholicism too became stronger. Some of the people, frightened and confused by the changing values that the Americans brought with them, turned again to Catholicism. Catholicism stood for Spain, for Spanish culture and tradition. Protestantism stood for America. Meanwhile the church itself was changing, influenced by the church in the United States.

Bishop James P. Davis, the Bishop of San Juan, a large, friendly, fatherly-looking priest, born in Houghton, Michigan, of Welsh and Luxemburger ancestry, told me one day in the three-hundred-year-old Bishopric House, "Yes, this is a Catholic country. About 80% of the country is Catholic—baptized as Catholics. But only about 20% are practicing Catholics."

The Catholic Church, here as everywhere, frowns upon contraception, sterilization, which is amazingly widespread especially among women, and all forms of family planning except for the rhythm method. Yet Puerto Rico actually has a law giving the Secretary of Health the right to give contraceptive advice and materials to anyone who asks for them. There are thirty-three Public Health Stations throughout the island where such information is available.

There is also an active Family Welfare Division Clinic headed up by a stout motherly-looking woman, Mrs. Celestina Zalduondo, whose volunteers go into the slums, the low-cost housing projects, and the communities in the hills, offering the services of the clinic. Working with the Worcester Foundation for Experimental Biology, the clinic is now carrying on a field test in the use of oral pills. "For three years," Mrs. Zalduondo told me, "we have been using these pills with 100% results. Not a single woman has become pregnant."

Bishop Davis, despite the fact that he is universally considered more friendly to the government than Brooklyn-born Bishop James E. McManus of Ponce, denounced both the government's attitude toward contraception and Mrs. Zalduondo's work in planned parenthood.

"It's not birth control that upsets me. It's the principle. The more powerful we become, the more we need the discipline of moral law. Otherwise we become a law unto ourselves. You can't legislate people out of existence. It's the difference between materialists and people with religion."

The Protestants have no scruples against planned families. In fact, Protestantism has made its inroads on the island by identifying itself with progress, with the new industrialization, and with the revolt against colonialism.

The religious picture in Puerto Rico is a fascinating and con-

Woman in a religious procession, San Juan Bautista Day, June 24

stantly changing one. Dr. Thomas A. Liggett, originally from
Florida, the tall, blond director of the "Seminario Evangélico de
Puerto Rico" in San Juan, told me: "The only religion that's really
aggressive and growing in Puerto Rico is Protestantism. So far as I
know this is the only country in Latin America, with the possible
exception of Chile, where Protestants comprise 10% of the population. Now while only 20% of the Catholics are practicing Catholics,
I would say that 80% of the Protestants are practicing Protestants."

   The Seminary, housed on a five-acre campus near the University
of Puerto Rico, is supported by Methodists, the United Presby-
terian Church, the Disciples of Christ, the American Baptists, the

Little girl in the San Juan Bautista Day religious procession

United Church of Christ, and the United Evangelical Church. Its school, started in 1919, trains young Puerto Rican men to become Protestant missionaries and ministers.

One of the most dedicated medical missions on the island, the Brethren Service Project in the mountains of Castañer, took in Nathan Leopold after his parole from prison, offered him complete protection from prying tourists, and a chance to become a useful citizen working as an X-ray technician in the hospital. There were stories that Leopold joined the mission as a convert. They are untrue.

When I first met Leopold in 1958, soon after his parole, he

looked like a visiting physician in a white jacket. He worked in a little laboratory in the mountain retreat doing X rays and taking blood-tests. He had the look of a man at peace with himself. He had not seen a child for thirty-three years. Now he was helping to heal children in the Brethren's hospital.

He was rediscovering the world in the mountains of this green island. One evening, relaxing in the warm home of Mayor José Barceló of Adjuntas, Leopold said revealingly, "I feel like a child."

A year later, Leopold knew how he could repay the Mission and the kindly poverty-ridden jíbaros who had accepted him with un-questioning hospitality. He would become a social worker so that through service he could help the people of the hills. He was given permission by his Parole Board to live in San Juan and study at the University of Puerto Rico. But the Mission at Castañer is his home and the jíbaros are the neighbors he hopes to heal.

The Brethren, whose missionary work is healing, have built a new hospital. Leopold, working with Doña Inés and the island's leading citizens, raised money so that this hospital could care for thousands of woefully needy people in the hills around Castañer.

Today almost anyone with a Bible and enough faith can become a lay leader and open a new church. In Puerto Rico the lay leader, with or without education, is an important figure in the hills and in the towns. Little stores become churches. You drive along the roads throughout the island and see little buildings suddenly springing up inviting the people of each barrio to leave the Catholic Church and find new emotional outlet among Holy Rollers.

Bishop Davis explained why the Pentecostals were making the deepest inroads in this once monolithically Catholic country. "The Puerto Rican men and women have a greater, deeper desire for some kind of religious experience than most other people. They are sitting ducks for anyone who has something exotic to offer. Catholic ritual has evolved through the centuries. It has achieved a certain form. It is too disciplined, too controlled, for the people who want to give vent to their emotions. The strongest Protestant Church here is the Pentecostal. They are the equivalent of the Holy Rollers. It is a truly native church. It doesn't depend on outside direction or help. The Catholic Church has suffered for years because there

The statue of Santiago Apostol, James the Apostle, the Spanish
warrior-saint, during the festival in Loíza Aldea, July 25

were too few priests here, about one priest to seven thousand
people. The Pentecostals have a lot of personal leadership. Their
leaders don't need to go to school. They've been to the school of
hard knocks."

There are said to be over a hundred thousand spiritualists
actively practicing the art of turning to the spirits, holding seances,
and listening to voices. The spiritualists are condemned both by

the Catholics and the Protestants. The Protestants call them pagan. The Catholics deny them the sacrament. Yet, according to Bishop Davis, "most of the spiritualists begin as Catholics, are baptized and confirmed, and then grow up thinking that they can combine spiritualism and Catholicism. Spiritism is deeply rooted in Puerto Rico and in Latin America. They had it here long before they were Christians."

A former newspaperwoman runs the Rossi Foundation in San Sebastian in the northwestern part of the island. She has a magnificent mansion in the hills with a tiny Sanctum Sanctorum, where she communes with her voices. Rossi is a healer. From all over the island the sick and the crippled are brought to her at $25 a visit to be healed by the spirits. Her detractors among the local townspeople of San Sebastian say that she has become a millionairess who rides around in a Cadillac, gets her followers to farm her land for nothing, and has never paid for anything but the first payment on her farm.

The newest religious group on the island are the "Mitas" (pronounced Meetas). They are the followers of Juanita García who calls herself "Mita," from Mamita—the little mother. According to some five thousand people she is the Messiah.

"I am the vessel through whom the Holy Ghost speaks," she said at a recent meeting in the temple she has built in Cantera, a workers' section of San Juan. The temple is a huge flat building with the name Mita blazoned across the front door.

"Moses is no higher than I am," Mita proclaimed. "Jesus is no higher. Through the ages the voice of God has returned to earth in human form. I am the last Messiah. The Day of Judgment will soon be at hand. Only my followers, the sinners who have repented and have taken Mita as their prophet, will be saved."

The people stood up and raised their arms to heaven. Each one said his personal prayers aloud, but quietly. Gentle old men with work-worn faces began to quiver in a frenzy. Some of the young girls lay on the floor, others rolled their eyes in repentance and salvation. These were good people and Mita was giving them something that filled their poverty-stricken lives.

Mita is a most unlikely-looking prophetess. She is a short, stout woman in her sixties with sallow skin and rimless glasses through which her dark brown eyes peer wisely. Her sparse white hair is pulled up into a tiny braid on top of her head; her features are plain with a goitrous neck. She dresses in a white linen Puerto Rican embroidered dress which wrinkles quickly in the tropical heat. "I am an ugly old woman," she says constantly in her sermons, plucking at her dress in disdain, "but the spirit of the Holy Ghost talks through me—*el Espíritu habla por mi*."

Like Father Divine, Mita preaches that her followers must be as pure and white as saints. The one hundred and forty-five "Mitas" who live with her in the two large houses she owns opposite the church must practice celibacy. Her followers give her everything they earn. In exchange Mita feeds them, houses them, gives them clothes for their jobs in the city, the white clothes they wear for the meetings held every Tuesday, Thursday, and Sunday night, the musical instruments for the fifty-man *"Banda de Mita,"* and the promise of redemption in the hereafter.

Like Rossi, Mita has her detractors. They say that she brings her followers to her farm in Arecibo on the northern coast every Saturday morning where they hold small meetings and do all her farm work for nothing. The Arecibo townsfolk who are not followers of the short, aging prophetess say that Mita has become a millionairess from the sweat of her followers.

The industrialization of Puerto Rico has built up a small Jewish community on the island. Many of them are the managers or owners of the new plants. Others are New Dealers who brought their skills as economists or lawyers or sociologists to the island, fell in love with it, and decided to stay. Still others have been on the island as owners of factories and businesses for forty years or longer. They have a synagogue on Ponce de León Avenue in San Juan in a beautiful old Spanish home surrounded by tropical flowers.

It was Doña Felisa who summed up, in a simple statement, the island's relaxed religion. At a convention of spiritualists one Sunday morning, Doña Felisa said, "My father was a spiritualist. My mother was a Catholic. They believed differently but they respected

and loved each other. That is why I have respect for everybody—
Protestants, Jews, Catholics, spiritualists—though I am a Catholic.
The failure of human beings is that sometimes, because they have
so much faith in their own religion, they cannot believe that people
with other religions are good."

CHAPTER 11

Operation Serenity

"I see—to resume—a culture based on work, peace of mind, on generosity; a people sheltered in modest but comfortable houses, satisfied with their tasks, secure against misfortune, possessed of abundant and simple food, happy in their recreation, without poverty; a land in which a man is esteemed for what he wants to do rather than for what he proposes to get; a community profoundly respectful of God and therefore free from spiritual conflicts."
—Muñoz Marín in a speech on March 3, 1952.

Serenity is the word. *Serenidad* is the yearning for culture, for good books, for music, for art, for peace of mind. Serenity is the promise of the future.

"Operation Serenity," Muñoz told me one day, "is mostly an affirmation of purpose—of not letting our civilization be blinded by economics as an end in itself. To create more personal freedom, deeper, better education—to make it possible for every citizen to have the chance to be just as good as God meant him to be."

The threefold Bill of Rights, dreamed up by Muñoz, has been carried through like the stages of a battle.

Operation Bootstrap was begun in the early 1940's to abolish poverty. It was more than new industries; it was health centers,

The University of Puerto Rico "Theatre on Wheels" on the road

schools, roads, hospitals, to lead the people up the long road out of hunger, sickness, and despair.

Operation Commonwealth came in the fifties, a new political form born of the island's economic needs.

Operation Serenity is the battle of the sixties. It is the battle for men's souls. Materialism alone is a dead-end street. It is not enough to give food to the hungry poor, not enough to raise their standard of living, not enough to give them political autonomy. They must live by spirit too. They must know what they want to make of themselves as human beings. They must try to shape their future not only in terms of decent houses with refrigerators and television, but in terms of spiritual energy and creative art.

Drama students of the University of Puerto Rico giving an outdoor
performance of *The Puppets of Cachiporra* by García Lorca

"Serenity," though it is less tangible than "Bootstrap" or "Commonwealth," gives deeper meaning to them both. "Its essential
meaning," Muñoz told me, "is that through political consciousness
and education, the people still realize that the economic effort is a
servant of the spiritual purpose and not an end in itself. You can
see Operation Serenity in the whole change that is taking place in
our country, materially and spiritually."

"Serenity" comes on wheels to the jíbaros in the hills. The best
musicians are sent around the island. A traveling library brings
books to everyone; a rolling museum brings art and history to the
most isolated community. One exhibit, rolled to the hills in a truck,

was made up of posters, pictures, old newspapers, and manuscripts showing the life and influence of the great Puerto Rican patriot, Luis Muñoz Rivera. Another exhibit was called "The 450th Anniversary of the Colonization of Puerto Rico." It had real Spanish coats of arms; wax models looked like Ponce de León's *conquistadores,* and the half-naked Indians whom they conquered.

The University of Puerto Rico sponsors a "Theatre on Wheels." On Sundays and holidays, a yellow, blue, and red stage truck drives to the central plaza of a town. Every man, woman, and child turns out to watch the actors who are either students of the University's Drama Department or apprentices from San Juan's junior and senior high schools. In the tradition of the road, the students make their own sets, paint them, act as stagehands, and finally come out on the boards of their open vans to perform Spanish translations of Shakespeare, Molière, Tennessee Williams, or Arthur Miller. Spanish classics are a favorite in the hinterland.

There is a ferment of government-sponsored culture. This is a government that knows that theatres need money, artists need money, musicians and symphonies need money.

Barry Yellen, a twenty-four-year-old New Yorker, started an American Theatre in San Juan a few years ago, and each year brings down plays with New York casts. His is a private enterprise, aided by the government, but most of the art and music is government-endowed. The Ballets de San Juan encourages and produces works by Puerto Rican composers; the Teatro de la Danza trains young dancers in the classical tradition of "Swan Lake" and "Don Quixote."

Puerto Rico's leaders are using the past to give the people pride in their culture. Under Spain and during the first years of American occupation, the study of Puerto Rican patriots was not stimulated. There was no complete history of Puerto Rico. Historical monuments were not protected; many were destroyed.

With the establishment of the Commonwealth, sprang the desire to preserve the cultural character of the Puerto Rican people. In 1955 the Legislature of the Commonwealth passed a law creating the *Instituto de Cultura Puertorriqueña,* the Institute of Puerto Rican Culture, whose purpose was to study, preserve and promote

Institute of Culture in Old San Juan

all aspects of Puerto Rico's national culture. Ricardo E. Alegría, a thirty-four-year-old anthropologist, was appointed director.

"The program of the Institute is very ambitious," he told me. "One of the most important projects is the preservation and restoration of historical zones and monuments. The old section of San Juan is under direct control of the Institute, which prevents the mutilation or destruction of the fine centuries-old Spanish architecture. Some of the beautiful houses with their beamed ceilings and inside arches have been turned into restaurants, guest houses, hotels, art galleries, dress shops, and museums."

An archeological site in the mountains of Utuado is being restored to show aboriginal culture; the ruins of Juan Ponce de León's house in Caparra are under restoration, to help understand the Spanish conquest and colonization of the island; Fort San Jerónimo, an eighteenth-century castle, just behind the Caribe-Hilton Hotel, has been restored to house a museum which shows

Porta Coeli in San Germán, a seventeenth-century church
now being restored as a religious art museum

the military history of Puerto Rico and its importance in the
defense of the Spanish Empire in America. The seventeenth-century church in San Germán, Porta Coeli, will be a religious art
museum. A house in old San Juan will show life in the capital a
hundred years ago.

Mr. Alegría, the tall, handsome son of an old and cultured
Puerto Rican family, is a Guggenheim fellow. He was working on
a Harvard Ph.D. and directing the Archeological Research Center
at the University of Puerto Rico when he was called to take this
job. He had to forget about his thesis and his Ph.D. In the spacious
halls of the Institute, he showed me some of the stone implements
of the earliest inhabitants, the "Archaic Indians" who lived on the
island 2,000 years ago. These were pre-ceramic and pre-agricul-

tural people; they were primitive nomads who probably came from Florida and migrated down the stepping stones of islands to Puerto Rico. There were excavations of the stone sculpture and pottery of the two other groups which came from South America about five hundred years after the "Archaics." They were the Igneris and Taino Indians, who had their origin in the jungles of the Orinoco.

Recently, President Eisenhower signed a law which will return to Puerto Rico all the historical documents which had been transferred to the National Archives of Washington during the first years of the American occupation. They are being housed in the Puerto Rican General Archives of the Institute, together with musical manuscripts of Puerto Rican composers, engravings, maps, and photographs.

"Although we are very much interested in preserving our cultural heritage," Mr. Alegría told me, "we are even more interested in promoting the culture of Puerto Rico today and in the future. But we believe that the experience and knowledge of the past can help us to project ourselves much better into the future."

Believing that cultural programs should not be limited to San Juan, the Institute has established cultural centers throughout the island. Concerts, lectures, documentary films, ballet, art exhibits, theatre, and the rolling museum appear in the small towns under the sponsorship of the Institute of Culture.

In the past, poetry was the art form in which Puerto Ricans distinguished themselves in world culture. The island has produced poets like Luis Llorens Torres, the poet of country life; Lola Rodríguez de Tió, a patriotic poetess; and the late Luis Palés Matos who used Negro themes in his writing. The Institute has now published a series of booklets of Puerto Rican poets, both living and dead, with illustrations by contemporary artists.

Today the island's most successful art form is the graphic arts. Most of the best-known Puerto Rican painters are working in government agencies, especially in the Division of Community Education and at the Institute of Culture. Their posters have won international recognition. Their paintings and sculpture are exhibited in the halls of the Institute and in small galleries all over

San Juan. New museums are opening rapidly; in Ponce, Luis Ferré recently opened a museum of fine arts in a restored Spanish colonial building, with a fine collection of old European painters.

To encourage young Puerto Rican dramatists and to promote the theatre arts, the Institute sponsors a Puerto Rican Theatre Festival at the charming pink Tapia Theatre in the Plaza Colón in San Juan. Plays by Puerto Rican authors portray the life, hopes, problems, and dreams of the island people. Now folklore ballets have been added to the Theatre Festival.

A unique place in Puerto Rico is La Casa del Libro, literally the House of the Book, on Calle del Cristo 255, a restored eighteenth-century house in old San Juan. The building, opened in 1958, is the brain child of a well-known bookman, Elmer Adler, who had built up the Graphic Arts Collection in the Department of Rare Books at Princeton.

The House of the Book, in beautiful Hispanic architecture, is on one of the narrow streets. It is only a few feet from the exquisite Cristo Chapel, built, according to the records, by a devout Puerto Rican in gratitude for the saving of the life of his nephew who, with his horse, had gone over the wall at the end of the street.

The exhibit which I saw was devoted to "Columbus and the Book." In well-designed glass showcases, fluorescently lighted, the books, some of which were duplicates of books Columbus had read, were displayed like jewels. There was a printed edition of Seneca with the page opened to *Medea*.

> Time will come in distant ages,
> When the ocean will reveal its mysteries
> An immense land will appear.

In another copy of this work, Columbus' son Ferdinand had written "This prophecy was fulfilled by my father, Christopher Columbus, in the year 1492."

Two *cédulas,* government decrees, displayed in another showcase were signed by the King and Queen of Spain, one on May 20, 1493, and the other on June 1, 1493. May 20th was the date of the decree of the appointment of Christopher Columbus as Captain

In La Casa del Libro

General of the fleet. The *cédulas* provided for wheat to provision
the fleet of seventeen ships being prepared for the voyage of discovery. It was on this second trip that Columbus discovered Puerto
Rico and named it San Juan.

How the *cédulas* came to rest in Puerto Rico, where they surely
belonged, was typical of the way Elmer Adler was building up the
collection in the House of the Book. There appeared a little item
in the press to report that he was planning this Columbus exhibit.
A dealer in England read the news, wrote Mr. Adler that he knew
of two important documents that were available, described them,
and said they were priced at £12,000—about $34,000.

The House of the Book had no such money. Mr. Adler wrote the dealer to ask if he could rent the documents. If later he could purchase them, then the rent could go toward the purchase price. The British dealer sent the documents to Puerto Rico. Mr. Adler examined them carefully, then showed them to Ted Moscoso, who had a constructive suggestion. Molinos de Puerto Rico was just about to start its flour and feed plant on the island. Mr. Moscoso told J. Allan Mactier, the President of Molinos, about the *cédulas* and the intriguing fact that they described flour which Columbus had needed to provision his fleet. Molinos bought the *cédulas* and presented them to the Puerto Rican people to be permanently kept in the House of the Book.

On the second floor of the Casa del Libro, metal library stacks hold nearly two hundred books printed before 1501. The collection, altogether totaling more than 4,000 volumes, includes some of the important editions of *Don Quixote*.

"Leather gets hungry," Mr. Adler told me, fingering one of the leather-bound books. "You have to keep feeding it. We make soup for the books, using the British Museum's formula."

Mr. Adler literally lives in, of, and for the House of the Book. He has an apartment on the second floor, right off the library. The furniture and most of the art collection on the walls of the reconstructed Spanish house are things he collected and brought from his house in Bucks County, Pennsylvania. Born in Rochester, New York, he traveled all over collecting books. In New York, interested in making good books, he became the organizer and designer of Pynson Printers, and one of the editors of *The Colophon,* the quarterly of bibliophiles.

Eating lunch in a restaurant in old San Juan, he told me the story of how the Casa del Libro was born. "In 1952, after twelve years with the Graphic Arts Collection in Princeton, I was retired upon reaching the age of 67. I spent one winter in New York and I didn't like the cold weather. In April 1955 I came to Puerto Rico to get the sun. A few people here knew that I had a little experience in printing, Ted Moscoso of Fomento, the Director of the Department of Education, and Guillermo Rodríguez who now directs one of the oil refineries. They invited me to lunch, and asked 'What can we do to improve the printing in Puerto Rico? We've discovered many talents among our people in industry, but somehow the art of good printing is something we haven't mastered.'

"I said, 'You have to show people good printing. People have to know there is good printing in the world. Puerto Ricans may never have seen well-designed, carefully made books. You can't develop good printers to print good books unless, from elementary school on, your children know about good printing. They don't see any examples. They should see.'

" 'How?'

"I suggested getting one of the old houses, restoring it beautifully, and then tying it up with its background. I'd collect the best examples of the beginning of printing, of printing through the ages, of modern printing. I'd put on exhibits that would arouse interest and understanding.

"Moscoso asked, 'Could you help us? Are you occupied now?' And, of course, I wasn't.

"He said, 'Can you stay a few weeks and help us get started?'

"I said, 'I'll come back.'

"I made certain arrangements. I insisted upon no salary. (Mr. Adler is still a dollar-a-year man.) I didn't want to be tied up with any organization. Actually, of course, Fomento, with the Department of Education and, later, the Institute of Culture, had to come in. I came back in the fall. They found an office for me. I began establishing connections. When I left Princeton, the library had agreed that when they began to catalogue my collection of special books, any duplicates would be available to me. I began to write letters. Contributions began to flow in. I happen to be one of the six honorary members of the Grolier Club of New York. I mailed one of our brochures to each of the members of the club. About a fifth of our collection so far has been contributions. In 1958 we started the *Amigos de Calle del Cristo 255*. The *Amigos,* or friends, is an association whose program is to enlarge the collection, increase the number of supporters, promote pilgrimages of all booklovers to the island, and to help increase the respect for Puerto Rico abroad, and show the people of Puerto Rico not only the art of printing but make them aware of what the book has contributed to civilization.

"This is the most satisfactory job I've ever had. It's creative.

Pablo Casals

You start with nothing and you have good expectations of winding up with something. The organization is already unique in South America. Of course in New York, you have three or four collections like this. But they're either connected with universities or they're privately operated. This collection belongs to the Commonwealth. It's especially important that it is a part of Puerto Rico."

For years the great cellist, Pablo Casals, had promised his mother who was born in Mayagüez that some day he would see her island. He kept that promise in 1956 at the age of eighty. Once he had seen the sunshine and beauty of the island, he decided this was where he wanted to live. He had been born in Spain, in Vendrell in the province of Catalonia, on December 29, 1876. Twenty-two years later, in 1898, the year that Puerto Rico became part of the United States, Pablo Casals won his first fame as a cellist.

He became a virtuoso with a passionate love of democracy. The civil war in Spain was his war, his war against fascism. In 1939, though he was in no danger from Franco, he left Spain as a voluntary exile, to protest to the world the rule of a man he considered evil. He lived in Prades, France, from 1939 until he came to Puerto Rico.

The Casals Festival in San Juan held each spring since 1957 has become world-famous. Though Casals suffered a heart attack that first year and could not play himself, his spirit filled the hall each night. The next two years Casals, with famous musicians such as Isaac Stern, Jan Peerce, Eugene Istomin, Alexander Schneider, and others brought new fame to Puerto Rico and new pride to its people.

At the age of eighty-four Casals formed the Puerto Rico Symphony Orchestra and the Commonwealth Conservatory of Music to train young Puerto Rican musicians.

In Puerto Rico he felt a freedom of spirit, a respect for the dignity of man. "I like the climate, both as to weather and politics. One cannot witness the degree of autonomy and self-government little Puerto Rico has without recognizing that here we have a relationship between a great power and a small state that is an example for the whole world."

Pablo Casals has come home.

CHAPTER 12

Who Goes to New York?

Early one morning a thirty-two-year-old man from the hills, his young wife, and their seven children ranging in age from seven years to three months, appeared at the ticket counter of Pan American Airways at San Juan's International Airport.

The man said in Spanish to the airlines agent, "You advertise— 'Fly now, pay later.' We want to fly now to New York."

The agent looked at the family of nine people and shook his head. He led the little group to the end of the concourse where a Traveler's Aid sign hung on the wall. Here Charlotte Hanson, one of the best social workers on the island, tall, gray-haired, sat at a desk with two social worker assistants.

The social workers talked with the man from the hills. He repeated his story. "Every day we hear that we should fly now, pay later. My sister is waiting for us in New York."

One of the social workers carefully explained that it was not really possible for them to fly now without paying.

"I will write a letter to your sister in New York," the social worker said, "and ask her to send you the money for the tickets."

The man was disappointed, but he agreed. "My sister has money. She will send it right away."

"The letter will take several days," the social worker said.

San Juan International Airport

"It does not matter. We will wait here."

By this time, some of the children were lying on the floor. The rest were sitting quietly, wide-eyed with attention, clinging to their mother. The mother sat silent in a strange world.

"You cannot stay here," the social worker said. "There is no place for the children to sleep. We will hire a car and send you home to your village."

"We cannot go home," the man said. "Everyone gave us a farewell party."

"They will understand."

"We put our *casita* (one-room house) up for sale this morning. Perhaps it is sold. We will stay here."

He looked around the airport. Hundreds of people were waiting for planes, waiting for relatives, weighing in their baggage. The airport was perhaps the busiest spot on the island. It was the nerve center of the migration.

All day the family stayed at the airport. The father had a little money with him. He bought some food for the children. He was a man of the world. He had been in New York once for two weeks. The mother had never been out of her native village before.

The day passed slowly. The children grew restless and tired. The three-month-old baby lay in its mother's arms, nursing or sleeping. The father looked content, certain that the letter would soon come from his sister in New York.

By five o'clock the mother, who had now seen the world, grew disturbed. She did not like to see her children lying tired on the floor. The night frightened her.

She spoke quietly to her husband. He returned to the social worker and said, "We will go home."

The Traveler's Aid hired a car and sent the family back to the hills.

A few days later the sister in New York sent them the money. They returned to San Juan and boarded a plane to the new world.

In the ups and downs of migration, the little family at the airport was not typical. Few families have migrated by pure caprice. Yet by now nearly every family in Puerto Rico has relatives on the mainland.

Who goes to the States? Is it the dreamers or the wastrels? Is it those who have no roots or those looking for streets of gold? Is it the dispossessed or those yearning to possess? Is it the wealthy or the poor, or the emerging middle class?

There were the families from the hills, families who had never even seen San Juan, who went right from the mountains in the hinterland into a huge plane that took them sixteen hundred miles northwest across the Atlantic to the excitement, the danger, the adventure, the bewilderment, and the sheer massiveness of New York.

There were also the more sophisticated Puerto Ricans who had lived in the cities of the island, in San Juan, in Ponce, in Mayagüez. They knew something of life in a metropolis.

"The best people go off," the Governor told me. "It's adventure.

It's pioneering. It's the fellow who would rather take a chance than stay home. Migration has been the most terrific force in the strength of the United States."

"It's not true that the Puerto Rican who goes to New York is the poorest and least desirable," Joseph Monserrat, the young director of the Migration Division's New York office, said. "Our statistics show that the migrants have a generally higher education and better skills to prepare them for life in New York."

New York has the same pull to Puerto Ricans that it had to the America-bound immigrants in the late nineteenth and early twentieth century. Their relatives are in New York; there is security in family. But the Commonwealth is trying to help them disperse across the country. Before 1948, 95% went to New York; now only 60% settle there.

This exodus differs from many other migrations in its youthfulness. Seventy-three per cent of the migrants are in the 15- to 44-year range. These are young people able to work, child-bearing people whose children may help supplement New York's labor supply. Of them, 25% come from the cities, San Juan, Ponce, and Mayagüez; 75% from rural areas.

"The people going to the States are a cross section of all Puerto Rico," Petroamérica Pagán de Colón, the over-all head of the Migration Division, told me. "About five years ago I began to find that people were going right from the rural areas of the island directly to the industrial cities and the farm areas of the States. Some become the spearheads and write home to their relatives and friends."

"But why do the people go?" I pressed her. "We know how much they love their island. Why do they leave home to live in a place where the climate is cold, the housing unbearable, and the inhospitality is often shocking?"

"The main reasons they go are for employment opportunities, better living conditions, schools for their children. Others go for emotional or environmental reasons. But the biggest group goes in search of work which they do not have here. The ones who go have ambition. They have revolted against the slums or against the part-time jobs in sugar cane during the *zafra,* the harvest, and

the hunger during the *tiempo muerto,* the dead time. Of course it
will be expensive for them in the States but they will begin to build
the standard of life they want for their children."

She described the job of orientation which the Migration Division was doing. "Here in Puerto Rico," she told me, "we try to
prepare migrants for their trip by telling them about the differences
they will find in life in the United States. We tell them what their
basic needs will be—in terms of food, housing, clothing, documents, jobs, language preparation. We tell them about the winter
and the type of clothing they need. We tell our people to be
careful, to keep their eyes open. We tell them that things in the
States may not be quite as good as they dreamed they were. We
tell them that the jobs they get may pay them more, but that their
money probably won't go as far. We even say that some of them
may not be as well off in the States as they are in Puerto Rico.
We do the best we can without painting a lurid half-true picture
of the life in the United States.

"We cannot tell them that all the houses in the States have rats,
but we tell them of the housing problems and of the difficulty in getting a good apartment and to take precautions so that they will not
end up with their family in a house infested with rats and cockroaches. We tell them that the best way to keep a house free of
rats and cockroaches is to dispose properly of the garbage and to
keep the place clean.

"We don't tell them that all employers take advantage of workers
to exploit them, but we tell them to be careful and to know the
agencies to which they should go in case they are paid substandard
wages. We don't tell them that all Americans harbor discrimination, but we emphasize the fact that many times, the race and color
of the skin make a difference as to where they will work or live.

"As American citizens we have a responsibility for the kind of
picture people all over the world have of the United States. We
believe that warning the people with too much emphasis against
the life in the United States is antagonizing them before they go
to the mainland. A person with a chip on his shoulder makes the
adjustment more difficult for himself.

"There are a few Puerto Ricans," she said, "who cause trouble for all the others by misbehaving. Their efforts toward achieving a better life are blocked, their dreams are frustrated; they become bitter, resentful, vindictive. The worst thing is that there is a tendency to judge all Puerto Ricans by the acts of this minority."

There is no question; most Puerto Ricans come to the States because their island cannot hold them. Despite Fomento, despite improved farming, the little island simply cannot feed 2,300,000 people. There are few natural resources; there are only people reproducing year after year.

Of some 450,000 families who live in Puerto Rico, there are still about 100,000 families for whom there is no peaceful revolution, no Fomento, no Operation Bootstrap, no serenity. There is misery and hunger and sickness and superstition.

Wherever you go there are people. You are surrounded on the beaches, in the streets, on the roads, in the hills, by people. Twenty years ago the exploding birth rate was offset by early death. In 1940, life expectancy was 46 years. Today it is 68 years; just two years less than the 70-year life expectancy of continental United States.

Ironically, if it weren't so good, it wouldn't be so bad. It is just because diseases are being wiped out, just because the life expectancy has increased by 47% since 1940, just because the infant mortality rate has gone down 41% and the death rate 60%, lower than any country in Latin America, that the island is more overpopulated than ever. Migration is an inevitable safety valve.

But the tragedy of many Puerto Ricans is that they love their land. They do not leave Puerto Rico because of political oppression, as many earlier immigrants came to America, fleeing terror or persecution or pogroms. They do not joyfully burn every political bridge behind them. They are proud Puerto Ricans, who have come to the mainland looking for jobs and food.

Digging roots into the mainland is more difficult for them than it was for many of the foreign immigrants who came in the nineteenth and the beginning of the twentieth century. Of all the newcomers, perhaps only the Italians and the Irish had the love and yearning for the homeland which the Puerto Ricans have. Those earlier immigrants too dreamed of returning to their homeland before they died. But the journey took a month of time and a lifetime of savings. To the Puerto Ricans, home is only three and a half hours away as the jet flies, and as cheap as a $45 economy flight.

To be sure, some come in the hope of earning enough money so that they can return, perhaps to buy a little house and open a little store in the towns in which they were born. European immigrants saved money so that they could bring their relatives here. So too the Puerto Ricans, out of their earnings, send money home either to bring relatives here or to help them remain on the island.

The people who say the United States should close its gates to Puerto Ricans apparently do not realize that Puerto Ricans are American citizens, and freedom of movement within our borders is a basic right. Coming to the mainland for a Puerto Rican is no different from an Iowan moving to Los Angeles or a Chicagoan retiring to Florida.

New York's Commissioner of Welfare, James R. Dumpson, at a conference of the American Public Welfare Association in Washington, D.C., in December 1959, said, "The Puerto Rican, particularly, has been singled out by those pressing for a residence requirement as a group of newcomers who increase welfare expenditures. Neither Puerto Ricans nor any migrant group come to a community for public assistance. . . . People move not for public assistance, but in search of employment; for better housing; for better educational opportunities. They move, too, in search of freedom from fear and for the opportunity to realize their full potential as individuals."

Certainly anyone who has driven through the hills of Puerto Rico, talked to the kindly jíbaros living a pastoral unhurried life in little wooden shacks, or watched the people in the mountains dressed in their Sunday best, clustering happily around their little country store, the *colmado,* listening to juke-box music which floods out to the road, or has seen a whole family at night in a one-room shack, the door wide open, securely absorbed in a television program, soon realizes the problems the Puerto Ricans face in adjusting to the hectic, competitive, pressure-ridden life of New York City.

A *colmado,* a country store

In the hills, the jíbaro lives in a small shack surrounded by sunshine, and air and green living things. When he washes his face in his bowl of water, he throws his water out of the window. He is sharing his water with the universe. But when he comes to New York and throws his water out of the window, it is not the universe. It is a slum on East 110th Street. Up in the hills, sitting under the stars, he doesn't worry about time. If he feels like singing at midnight, he sings and he disturbs no one. But in New York, if he sings at midnight, he will probably be waking ten families who have to get up at six the next morning.

Yet Puerto Ricans have adjusted faster to New York in ten years than most immigrant groups have adjusted in a whole generation. Governor Muñoz analyzed this swift adjustment one evening as we sat at dinner in his mountain retreat at Jájome Alto. "I think that Puerto Ricans have adjusted faster because there's a closer political relationship between Puerto Rico and the United States than there was between any of the countries that earlier groups came from.

"Some day," the Governor said, "I hope to spend about three weeks living in New York incognito, and see how the Puerto Rican people are living, and get a spontaneous relationship with them."

A few years ago, the Governor's wife spent such a day in New York, although it was as difficult for her to be incognito among the thousands of people who love her as it would be for her husband. In fact, a man, dressed as a peanut in an advertising stunt, called to her in Spanish, "Hello, Doña Inés. Look at me. I'm in New York as a peanut, earning my rice and beans."

She walked around East Harlem with Reverend Norman Eddy of the 100th Street Church, visiting rat-infested slums.

"I am sick at what I saw," she told me one evening in San Juan. "I think we should try to keep our people here. It is a terrible destiny for people to emigrate. It breaks my heart. They are better off in Puerto Rico. They have schools here, milk stations, everything—but not enough work. They talk of progress when they go to New York. But I know what they are going through for progress. They are warm and kind people. But look what happens to them in New York.

"Gangs prosper in New York partly because there the young people try to go out of their anonymous existence. They become a kind of Robin Hood—to get publicity, to get their pictures in the papers. Here our boys are not anonymous. A seamstress is a very respected person here. Her son is a very respected person. The family is very strong. In New York, family life is broken. The woman usually gets the first job—in needlework. If the husband doesn't get a job, he deteriorates. In New York he is no longer the head of the family. The children begin to leave the house. How can they live in that terrible housing? People make fine conciliatory speeches. That is not enough. Now is the time to be strong and

Jaime Gonzalez, a thirty-six-year-old barge-loading foreman
at a midwest steel mill

honest. They have to enforce the law on the landlords. We need leaders, real leaders, who will live right among the people and teach them to help themselves. That's what they are doing in Puerto Rico and that's what we must do in New York. It doesn't matter whether the leaders are white or Negro or Puerto Rican. It just matters that they help our people to help themselves."

A short time ago a survey was made to determine where Puerto Ricans have settled in the States and what they are doing. They are working with explosives in the copper mines of Utah; they are among the elite of the miners, the dynamiters, truck drivers and steam-shovel operators who had come after World War II and stayed. They are working in the marble quarries in Vermont. A large colony of Puerto Ricans is in Hawaii.

In Youngstown, Ohio, in Bethlehem, Pennsylvania, in Lorain, Ohio, in Gary, and in Chicago where there are now 25,000 Puerto Ricans, they are working in the steel foundries; they are in leather tanning, shoe manufacturing and electronics in Milwaukee, in automobiles in Detroit, in men's clothing in Rochester, in radio and television manufacture in northern New Jersey.

In New York where some 690,000 Puerto Ricans have settled (212,000 of that number born in New York), they are in manufacturing industries; they own their own grocery stores, barber shops, drug stores. They are physicians, dentists, lawyers, teachers, and policemen.

"What should we do *with* the Puerto Ricans?" someone is said to have asked in New York. "What would we do *without* the Puerto Ricans?" was the answer.

If there were no Puerto Ricans, we would have to create them. It is the Puerto Ricans who have kept the needle-trade industry alive in New York City. Without the Puerto Ricans, we would have to search for a new labor force to replace the Jewish and Italian garment workers who came at the turn of the century and whose children have become white-collar workers or professional men.

There are more Puerto Ricans employed in the garment trade in New York than in all the Fomento industries in Puerto Rico. Forty-six thousand Puerto Ricans, famous for their dexterity and finger skills, are now making the dresses and suits for consumers all over the nation.

"If not for the Puerto Rican influx, the garment industry would have left New York," says the head of Local 148 of the International Ladies Garment Workers Union.

The vice-president of the Art-Steel Corporation in the Bronx, Irving McKinley Levy, told me that 80% of his labor force is made up of Puerto Ricans. "Without our 600 Puerto Ricans," he says, "we would have to close shop."

New York's $460,000,000 hotel business would be endangered. "The Waldorf-Astoria could not run without its 450 Puerto Rican workers," the personnel director of the Waldorf has said. Restaurants would close. Hospitals would close. Many of the hospitals say that some of their most devoted nurses are young Puerto Rican women.

Ours is a world in flux. Since the end of World War II, over thirty-five million people have been uprooted by the tragedy of war or rising nationalism.

In the United States alone, five million people migrate from state to state each year in search of jobs or better homes. The Puerto Ricans represent less than 1% of that number. Their adjustment to life on the mainland is that of almost every migrant group today, whether it be the southern mountaineer adjusting to city life in Cincinnati or the Negro from South Carolina adjusting to Chicago.

Farm people move to cities that have no houses to shelter them. Schools, police facilities, parks, recreation clubs are taxed beyond capacity. These are the problems of all migrations. In our time, the Puerto Ricans have become their personification.

The Puerto Ricans did not create the problems on the mainland; they inherited them. They did not create the slums; they were allowed, for the most part, only to move into buildings that were already deteriorating. They work at jobs in New York, but often their wages cannot feed a large family, so the Welfare Department gives them supplementary relief for dependent children.

The big exodus of Puerto Ricans to the States began at the end of World War II as employers searched for labor, and airplanes squeezed the world so that Puerto Rico was at New York's back door. As with every wave of migration, the Puerto Ricans were met with hostility.

The Puerto Rican Government decided to do what no state or nation had ever done, follow its people to New York and try to help them adjust. In 1948, the branch of the Labor Department, called the Migration Division, was set up in New York and later in ten other cities. New York City began to recognize its own responsibility and in September 1949, Mayor William O'Dwyer created the "Mayor's Advisory Committee on Puerto Ricans." Civic and community leaders, among them the leading Puerto Ricans in New York, planned together for the education, health, and welfare of the new arrivals.

The schools became a focal point. The city recognized that educating the children of the newcomers was the first step in helping the Puerto Rican family adjust to the new life.

NES (Non-English-Speaking) classes have been set up in the schools to teach English to the Puerto Rican children, and to help those who know English overcome their timidity. Many come north knowing English but with a thick Spanish accent that has often unfortunately been taught to them on the island. The teachers in the NES classes work hard on pronunciation and even harder on instilling confidence. Many of the children, especially those with dark skins, continue speaking Spanish in the school yards and on the street because they want to be identified as Puerto Ricans, not as Negroes.

The Board of Education has set up a special category of teachers who are Puerto Ricans themselves. Called SAT (Substitute Auxiliary Teachers), they are the liaison between the school and the home. They interview the parents whose children are being registered; they translate for parents who come to school for any reason at all; they work closely with the Spanish-speaking children.

Each summer, about a hundred teachers, supervisors, and social workers from predominantly Puerto Rican neighborhoods are sent on scholarships to the island. In a briefing given by the Board of Education before they go, they are told the purpose of their mission—to learn the truth about Puerto Rico and the Puerto Ricans so that they may better understand their pupils and the families whom they must counsel.

The teachers' scholarships are paid for jointly by the Board of Education, the National Conference of Christians and Jews, and the University of Puerto Rico. New York University runs a workshop of its own in San Juan. At the Inter-American University at San Germán, Cornell University conducts a workshop for teachers from all over New York State and its environs. The Catholic

University at Ponce sponsors a workshop for nuns and religious leaders. Under the direction of Dr. Harold Fields, the Graduate School of Education of Yeshiva University has been holding workshops in New York since 1958. Social workers are given scholarships for a social workers' summer workshop on the island by the University of Puerto Rico and the Migration Division of the Labor Department.

But the work done in the schools and by public and private agencies is for the most part done by non-Puerto Ricans. The Puerto Ricans have lacked grass-roots leadership. They have little experience and no background in community responsibility. Many still think, like the jíbaros, in terms of the family as their social security.

In the hills of Puerto Rico, family social security is a positive thing—a source of survival. But in urban living, family responsibility needs to be enlarged to include the block, the neighborhood, the community, the city, and ultimately the world.

To many of the newcomers, urban living is as strange as it was to the people who came out of the Irish potato fields, the Italian farms, or the medieval-like villages of Poland and Russia. Some of them must be taught the simple hygiene of putting a lid on a garbage can, of nailing up a rat-hole, of keeping a hallway or a city street clean.

Teachers and social workers can point up the importance of community living. But the realization of their own responsibility is the problem which the Puerto Ricans themselves must face.

It may take carefully chosen men and women, trained on the island, to come out of Puerto Rico and live for a year or two in different neighborhoods, developing self-help and genuine grass-roots leaders.

A more immediate solution is an increasing shouldering of responsibility by the earlier Puerto Rican arrivals who have made good on the mainland. Some of them have already begun helping the newcomers by combining their knowledge and understanding of the Puerto Ricans with the good will and know-how of the non-Puerto Rican leaders of neighborhood and community councils.

In East Harlem, Pedro Canino, who worked for thirty-four years in the Post Office in New York, helped set up an organization descriptively called the "East Harlem Civic Orientation Center." He gives advice; he helps the children in school and the parents in jobs and housing; on Thanksgiving and Christmas he goes around the neighborhood bringing food baskets to the hungry. In February 1960, he retired from the Post Office to become a full-time volunteer helping his people to help themselves. They call him "The Mayor of East Harlem."

The New York-Puerto Rican Scholarship Fund sends Puerto Rican boys and girls, who qualify but lack the funds, to college so that they may return to the community as leaders.

On New York's West Side, the Riverside Neighborhood Assembly, made up of both Puerto Rican and mainland community leaders, has set up a "Pride-in-Neighborhood" program. Its purpose is to get strangers who happen to live near each other to participate in neighborhood activities, to take "pride" in the streets they live on. Under its president, Stanley H. Lowell, former Assistant to Mayor Robert Wagner, the RNA works directly through the children in the neighborhood, reaching them for the most part through their schools.

Recently the American Friends' Service Committee bought a condemned four-story brownstone at 94 East 111 Street, a street almost wholly Puerto Rican, with brownstones and Spanish names on every store. Ten young volunteers moved into various houses on the block, all working full-time during the day as teachers or social workers outside the block. The two leaders of the group, Dan Murrow and his wife, Hope, both social workers, live in a tiny apartment on the fourth floor of the house itself, with their new-born baby, Claudia.

Most of the Friends' neighborhood work is done on week ends. College students, many of them from upper-middle-class homes in greater New York and New Jersey, come to live at the house for "week-end work camps." On Friday nights, they have discussions on all phases of the problems of adjustment; on Saturday they go into the block and work with the Puerto Rican families in the tenements, plastering, painting, fixing door jambs, cementing rat holes. They go only to the apartments of neighbors who have

Pedro Canino, "The Mayor of East Harlem"

come to the Friends asking for help; the landlords supply the materials, the families and the young college volunteers supply the work.

One day in July 1959, when the problem of gangs was a daily front-page story, the leader of the Viceroy Gang went to Dan Murrow. The boys, he said, were tired of warfare, of not being able to walk on each other's turfs, of not knowing how soon they would get killed. He asked Murrow to set up a council of all the gangs in the neighborhood.

More than twenty gangs responded. They called themselves the "East Harlem Youth Council." They met at the Friends' house every two weeks. They mediated before each other. They elected as their chairman John Torres, a tall twenty-three-year-old boy who had been to a reformatory and back. He has innate intelligence, but not much schooling. He decided it was crazy to live the way he had been living. "I have seen guys die, go to jail, get hurt bad. I can't forget."

The gangs declared a "cool." They worked out a new pattern in the youth life of their neighborhood. All turfs were eliminated. Guns and knives were banned. Working with the Youth Board, the boys began to help their neighbors paint apartments and clean up the block.

In August 1958, an organization called United Puerto Ricans was formed with a number of leading Puerto Rican professional and business people in New York. Its president is Fini Rincón, Doña Felisa's sister. Run completely by volunteers, with Judge Anna Kross, New York's Commissioner of Corrections as Honorary President, the United Puerto Ricans is organizing volunteers to go into the hospitals and the prisons, especially the Women's House of Detention, in a kind of volunteer welfare role.

In the South Bronx, in September 1959, the City of New York set up a "Community Action Program—St. Mary's Neighborhood Project." Its purpose is to try to prevent and control juvenile delinquency through indigenous leaders in a neighborhood called picturesquely, St. Mary's, a low-income area with a mixed population of Puerto Ricans who are in the majority, and Irish, Negroes, Italians, and Jews.

"In an area like ours," Dr. William Jackson, the director, told me, "the need for motivating the community toward self-help is paramount. CAP rallied the neighborhood as a whole to marshal its resources for the care and protection of its children and families.

"We use the block organization approach. We've had an unusually enthusiastic response from the Puerto Rican residents as volunteers in the organization of the area block by block. They are serving as block leaders, interviewers for surveys, committee members, etc.

"In a few months, we began to see a trend away from self-improvement (individual and group) to neighborhood improvement. Recently the Puerto Rican Self-Help Committee co-operated with CAP in setting up a Community Housing Clinic. It is manned by a bilingual lawyer and other community volunteers."

The Puerto Rican Self-Help Committee, organized in September 1959, represents 162 Puerto Rican organizations in the city who want not only to fight delinquency but to give "non-Spanish-speaking citizens a better understanding of their fellow citizens of Puerto Rican background."

One of its first acts was to set up a "credo" for parents through the Spanish press and radio to remind parents of the importance of knowing the whereabouts of their children at all times, of keeping in close touch with their children's teachers, and if they sensed any trouble, to seek guidance from their church or from social workers and other agencies.

The President of the Self-Help Program is also the Director of the Migration Division of the Labor Department, Joseph Monserrat. "There is a tremendous dynamic and cultural life being lived by Puerto Ricans in New York," he told me. "There are constant exhibitions of paintings done here by Puerto Ricans or sent up from the island. There are Puerto Rican plays produced in Spanish. Two groups of young people are struggling to develop off-Broadway theatres. Among our people are actors and directors like José Ferrer; there is Graciela Rivera, the opera singer; there are baseball players like Vic Power and Orlando Cepeda, and scores of successful engineers, lawyers, doctors, carpenters, prize-fighters, masons, and cooks."

The Puerto Ricans are here to stay. The problems their coming presents will disappear in the next few decades, if they are met with patience and honesty.

Time and education are on the side of the second generation. There are already some two hundred thousand second-generation Puerto Ricans who have their own contribution to make to life on the mainland.

"My father," one of them said to me in New York, "would never agree that he should have stayed in Puerto Rico, instead of coming here when I was a baby, and giving me my chance to go to college. Nor would the fathers of my friends who are engineers or Air Force pilots. Sure we began in the slums. But I don't know that the slum left a mark on me. I think the fire-escape education made it possible for me to understand my people better and to help them.

"Yet even we second-generation Puerto Ricans know what prejudice means. My six-year-old daughter is dark-skinned. She came home from school one day and said, 'Daddy, why am I different?' "

He swallowed hard as he said it. "Maybe that's why I'm working so hard for the Puerto Ricans coming here now, so that their sons and daughters and my daughter's daughter won't have that kind of wound."

CHAPTER 13

The Jíbaros Build a Bridge

Summer lingers long in Puerto Rico, long after it is autumn and winter on the mainland. On a warm September evening we drove to a small community of one hundred and twenty-five families living in the hills. They called their community "Francés"; they were near Vega Alta, about thirty miles west of San Juan.

We were driving in a station wagon with Fred and Carmen Wale who, through "Community Education," were helping to bring the new Puerto Rico into the mountains. Fred Wale is a mainlander, a lean, graying idealist who had been a teacher's teacher in the States; he had worked for the Farm Security Administration and the Julius Rosenwald Fund. Fred's wife Carmen is a Puerto Rican, with golden skin; black, sparkling, compassionate eyes; wavy black hair and a strong face. She is a career woman, a former social worker and the mother of a four-year-old daughter, Carmencita.

Several nights a week Fred and Carmen, who head up the Division of Community Education, closed their office in old San Juan, left Carmencita with a relative, and drove in their station wagon to the hills to join a field worker of the Division as he sat with a group of people, discussing their problems.

It was a purely Puerto Rican picture. For months and even years, idealistic men, called group organizers, working with Car-

A roadside store in the hills

men and Fred in the Division of Community Education, got into jeeps and traveled to the hills. There under the blue Puerto Rican skies they sat outdoors with the people and talked things out.

Beyond Vega Alta, our station wagon began climbing a winding dirt road. The tiny wooden houses of the jíbaros were tucked into hollows. Little children sat in front of the houses talking quietly. Chickens ran freely, squawking. Birds flitted through the trees, their voices full-throated. Night had fallen swiftly and gently. Some of the houses had a spot of yellow light from a kerosene lamp. Other houses were already dark. But lighted or not, by kerosene or candles, each house had quiet children on the steps of the porch, watching us drive by.

I suddenly realized that I had never seen boisterous children in the hills of Puerto Rico. They might be playing, singing, talking to each other, watching life go by on the road. But always they were quiet and well-behaved. Yet these were the same kind of children whose families took them directly from the hills to San Juan's International Airport and on to New York—to a new life in the turbulent slum-ridden ghettos that tonight seemed like another planet.

"Donde es la reunión?" "Where is the meeting?" Fred asked an attractive dark-haired woman who was walking with her daughter. She pointed further up the hills and then joined us in the car to drive the rest of the way.

Gradually we could see a light shining through the trees. We drove toward it. In the middle of a clearing was a bare bulb strung up on top of a long, thin iron pole stuck in the ground. Chago, the group organizer, had strung it up and attached it to the electric generator in his jeep. As we drove closer we could see two spotlights which he had placed on the wall of a building under construction.

About seventy people had come to the meeting. Some thirty of them sat on children's folding chairs in a circle around the pole of light; some forty more stood behind the chairs, their faces catching a little of the light. In the background under a tree stood a group of young married women, a few of them pregnant, others holding their little children by the hand.

Even in the inner circle of chairs, there were a number of children, little girls in cheap but clean cotton dresses, sitting silent and composed as though they had been rigidly disciplined. Yet the Puerto Ricans hardly ever discipline their children. What made them so well-behaved, particularly at this hour? For it was already 7:30 and the hills had lost their contours in the darkness. I knew that the Puerto Ricans in the hills, like the Eskimos in the tiny Arctic villages in Alaska, showered their children with love. They never seemed to use a harsh voice to their children; you heard them whispering to them softly; you saw them kissing their babies;

you saw them walking hand in hand with their children through the hills. The child was the center of the family; and the family, large, closely knit, and happy, was the center of the community. Yet surely love alone could not be the answer. I had seen too many families in the States and in Europe lavish love on their children, and still some of the children turned into delinquents. Was it the close-knit family in the Puerto Rican hills? Was it the lack of the big-city pressures and tensions? Was it the respect for their parents that was inbred in Puerto Rican society?

I looked at the faces of the parents and grandparents and the young unmarried boys and girls in their teens and early twenties. The old men in freshly washed jeans, with open-collared shirts and panama hats, sat silent, looking like religious *Santos*—the wooden saints carved by the *Santeros* in the hills. The *Santeros* were wood-carvers whose only carvings were of saints. They were the newly discovered primitives in Puerto Rican folk art.

The young men looked like farmers in the States, their strong faces freshly scrubbed, their black hair brushed back, most of them in colorful washed shirts which they wore like jackets over their jeans.

There were three or four old women with parchment faces and dark eyes that showed a thousand years of wisdom. But at least a third of the group were young girls in smart attractive dresses and gay earrings, their lips bright with scarlet and fuchsia lipstick, their black hair brushed like smooth satin into gay pony tails or loose curls. Most of the girls worked during the day in the large Remington Rand plant in Vega Alta. While they waited for the meeting to begin, they talked animatedly to each other, and broke into quick laughter.

The group organizer, whom everyone called Chago but whose name was Santiago Narvaez, walked among the people. He looked like the jíbaros. He was dressed like them. He was thin, with a mobile, high-cheeked face.

Now he sat down on one of the little folding chairs and without any speeches, he said simply, "We are going to start tonight with a game."

He called on one of the younger men who came to the pole of

light. The young man said, "I will guess the thoughts of three people here."

He chose three more young men, asked them to stand beside the light, put three small things on the ground in front of them, made two of the men go back to their places around the circle, and kept one of the men at the light.

"Remember," the first young man said, acting now like a vaudevillian on amateur night, "I have no eyes in my back." Then he turned his back and told the man at the pole to move one of the three things on the ground.

The man at the pole said, "Now tell me, what thing did I move?"

The jokester said, "Your tongue."

The community laughed quickly. This was the warming up.

Now the community education meeting was under way. Chago opened a carton of books in front of him and handed out copies of a red, paperback book on whose cover were four strong Puerto Rican faces looking across the turquoise hills into the rising sun. The book was called *Juventud*—Youth. In the meeting only those who knew how to read took copies. Later there would be a book in every home. The old *Santos* listened, their eyes looking straight ahead, their thoughts turned inward.

A girl who looked about eighteen, with laughing dark eyes, white skin, and a cameo-face like one of Goya's Majas, began the reading in Spanish.

"Qué es juventud? Juventud, divino tesoro; ya te vas para no volver."

"Youth is in the spirit," she read in Spanish. "Youth is not lost when wrinkles furrow the face, or white streaks cover the head, if the spirit of youth is conserved. The fountain of youth is not in Florida where our Ponce de León went in search of it. The fountain of youth is in ourselves, in the depths of our being."

The book was made up of short stories, poems by well-known Spanish and Puerto Rican poets, games, tricks of magic, anecdotes of the great past leaders of the island and *"pensamientos"*—philosophical reflections of Confucius and Rabindranath Tagore.

When the young girl reader read a line saying "Youth should not stop progressing," Chago quietly asked the young people around the circle, "Do you feel you have done that?"

A young man with a warmly intelligent face nodded his head. He was the volunteer librarian for the community. He had a revolving library bookcase in his home. The neighbors came to him in the evenings after work to borrow books. He even spent time in San Juan with other volunteer librarians attending seminars in the Library Program of the Department of Education.

"I think we are progressing. Our youth are working. We are studying. We are trying to improve our lives." He spoke simply but with great warmth. You knew somehow that he was one of the new young leaders. His roots were deep in these hills. He would help lead his people up the road.

This was the way a people learned pride in their history, pride in themselves. Here was something worked out in Puerto Rico. In Alaska, in the Canadian Arctic, and in the Arab world, I had seen people meet together in tribal meetings, council meetings, religious meetings. But there was a unique quality here that seemed born of these hills, rooted in the love of "patria," of their country, of Puerto Rico.

Governor Luis Muñoz Marín, in one of the famous Godkin lectures at Harvard University in April 1959, described "patria" as "the colors of the landscape, the changes of seasons, the smell of the earth wet with fresh rain, the voices of the streams, the crash of the ocean against the shore, the fruits, the songs, the habits of work and the leisure, the flowers, the typical dishes for special occasions and the austere ones for every day, the valleys, the pathways; but even more than these things, 'patria' is the people, their way-of-life, spirit, folkways, songs, the way of getting along with each other. Without these things 'patria' is only an abstraction, a piece of scenery. With them it is an integral whole, the homeland *and* the people."

Here in this circle of neighbors you suddenly understood that wisdom, that pride in their land. In the hills they were helping themselves to better the "patria." To make life more comfortable. To solve the problems of daily living.

Each of the communities talked their problems through at their fortnightly community education meetings. Some needed a bridge.

A Community Education poster announcing
a competition for the best *Santos*

Some needed a road. Some needed a schoolhouse. The community of Francés had discussed for months what they needed most. They had many needs. They had no electricity. They had no running water. Far down the hill in the barrio, the ward, there was a public faucet. The women and children walked long distances carrying the water from the faucet in pails on their heads up the hills to their little wooden houses.

A few months before we visited Francés, the people decided that water was their greatest problem. There was not enough money to bring water to every house. Little by little the *Santos,* the strong-faced young farmers, the pretty young girls, and the idealistic young men thought through and said aloud what the leaders of this revolution in Puerto Rico hoped they would say, "This is our community. We are the first ones who have the right and the responsibility to think about it. If it is not possible to bring us the water immediately, then perhaps we can help ourselves. We will build our own water system and we'll ask the government for the help we cannot ourselves give."

Obviously they could not do it alone. They needed engineers to help them. They knew nothing about aqueducts and pipe lines, and they would need some financial help. And this they sought.

Several weeks before we came, they sat in their circle around the unshaded bulb, listening to an engineer from the Aqueducts Authority. He told the people what the project would mean. They would get their water from the aqueduct at Vega Alta. There were already pipes laid in the main highway. The people of Francés would have to connect the pipes from the main line to their homes. In terms of engineering, this was a simple project, he said. But in terms of time and man power and especially of material, it was expensive: they would need long pipes to bring the water up the mountains. The neighbors would have to dig trenches eighteen inches deep to lay the pipes and then cover them up.

In the next weeks the engineers estimated the total cost of the project. It was high; to most of the jíbaros it seemed fantastically high. It would cost about $20,000 to bring water to their homes. More meetings took place around the pole of light.

The people studied the budget. A mimeographed copy was given to every home for every member of the family. Then the community decided all that it could give—money (collections were made), land, tools and, the most important of all, the unskilled labor and some of the skills for the entire project. When this had been determined they visited the mayor and he promised to help with $1,000 for the purchase of materials.

About this time a sum of $6,000 was assigned by the Legislature to bring water to their community. The Governor, knowing that it was not enough to complete the job and knowing also of the effort of the people of Francés, signed the bill with the understanding that it would be used to match the people's resources.

The people of Francés began working. They worked mostly on Saturdays and Sundays. Every two weeks they made new work teams for the next fifteen days. The men put in five hundred man-days of work, free. The work progressed until they had used up the $6,000. They got another $3,000 from the Economic Fund of the Department of Public Works. Then suddenly they had to stop. Something was delaying the $1,000 promised by the mayor. At a meeting which had taken place two days before we visited them, the people decided not to wait any longer. They would apply again to the Economic Fund. They were sure that with the last $1,000 and their own resources they could finish their project.

However, at tonight's meeting Chago announced that the grant from the mayor was available and plans for the resumption and completion of the project could continue. One of the men, Alfredo, stood up behind one of the chairs and began to talk. He began slowly and soon grew excited. He wore city clothes and a gray hat with a striped ribbon around it. He lived here and worked as a mechanic in San Juan.

"Don't bother me with the budget and with figures," he told Chago angrily. "Tell me what happened to the $6,000."

The people listened quietly while Alfredo talked, his words carefully implying that someone had stolen some of the money. Perhaps it was the engineers. The honesty of the government was in question.

Alfredo had brought supporters with him. One was a young man, dressed not like the farmers but in a city jacket. He began to talk.

I could not tell at first whether he was disturbed, excited, or drunk. But soon it became clear that he was drunk. His voice had a catch in it as if he were crying. Some of the people cast their eyes on the ground, ashamed at one of their neighbors. Others laughed good-naturedly.

Carmen entered the debate. Her fine face with its golden skin and dark eyes, lighted by the single bulb, was filled with warmth. Carmen explained that people have a right to question and that it would be very easy to invite the engineers to a meeting to give the neighbors a complete progress report. Then they would know the truth.

The young drunk, who had disappeared behind the trees, came back now, talking loudly. "You're all fools. You lick everyone's feet. You work for nothing and these people get the money. You remind me of a story." He kept touching his fingers to his right cheek. "When the Lord was making animals, He made the rooster. Before He gave the rooster teeth He got tired. So He decided to wait until morning to give him his teeth. But the rooster was so pleased with his beak that in the morning he said to the Lord, 'I like my beak so much I can eat anybody. I can eat you, too.'

"Then the Lord said, 'I better not give you any teeth because if you feel that way now without teeth, who knows what you would do with teeth?' "

The neighbors laughed at his joke, though he, too, was implying that there had been shady deals in the project. The evening ended. The neighbors would meet again in two weeks. They knew there was no skulduggery. They knew Alfredo and his supporters. They would work, against all obstacles; they had to bring water to their homes. Then they would find another project—perhaps a bridge.

As we drove home in the station wagon I remembered a talk I had had months before with Carmen and Fred. Fred, who always talked poetically, in a kind of free verse, said then, "The road, the school, the bridge, are not the end. It is the spirit that is the end. It is the process of growth, the growth of people. The solution of a problem is an expression of growing, not its purpose."

Now in the quiet darkness of the Puerto Rican night, the im-

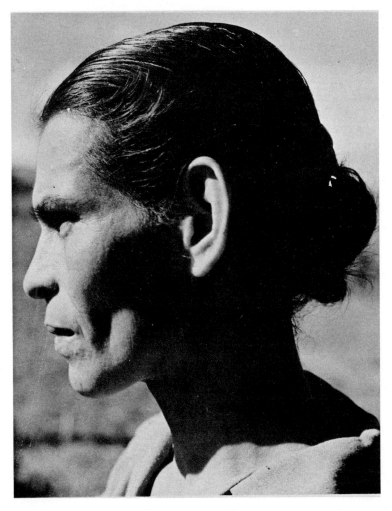

A rural woman

portance of the water project in the whole development of the
people struck me as a crucial issue. I suddenly felt that they must
complete this project, not only so that every overworked mother
in a little shack would know the miracle of turning a faucet, but

so that the young girl with the Maja face who had read, "Youth is in the spirit," and the old *Santos* would not be betrayed.

"If the community project is not an end in itself," I said, "if bringing water to their homes is not an end in itself, then what is the end?"

Fred answered. "The community project is a landmark. The pipeline, the bridge, the school, the roads are landmarks. Inside themselves the people are building a road on which they are moving along; the landmarks are along the way."

It was the spirit then that was the end. It was "Serenity" giving meaning to "Bootstrap." It was the people who had lived on their beautiful island in poverty, looking toward the morning. It was the squatters building their own homes, with refrigerators and television sets. It was the landless getting land. It was the workers in the bright new industries walking with pride. It was the wise but uneducated learning to read. It was man growing whole again through his own inner strength.

CHAPTER 14

Puerto Rico Is Like Israel

Puerto Rico and Israel are startlingly alike.

Both are new democracies on old soil.

Both are pulling themselves up by the bootstraps with the same dynamic and creative spirit. Both countries, still underdeveloped lands, have begun their own Point Four programs to teach other underdeveloped lands the exciting things that each has learned through trial and error.

Both have strong ties to the United States, and stronger and more emotional ties to the people of New York than to any other city in the world.

Each country is led by a man who is a dreamer, an idealist, a statesman, and a shrewd hard-headed politician who controls his party completely.

Luis Muñoz Marín, the chief architect of Puerto Rico's Operation Bootstrap, became the island's first elected Governor in 1948. David Ben-Gurion, the chief architect in the re-creation of Israel, became Israel's first Prime Minister in the same year.

Both are strong men in a hurry. Both are philosophers who need constantly to withdraw from the madding crowd to find themselves again, to think, to be purified and regenerated. Ben-Gurion goes to the desert; Muñoz goes to the mountains.

Both are prophetic men, poets deeply concerned with ideas and words. Ben-Gurion at 60 was studying Greek to read the classics, and at 70 was studying Spanish to read Cervantes. "To read the classics in translation," he once told me, quoting the Hebrew poet Bialik, "is like kissing a woman through a veil."

Muñoz who was a free-lance writer in Greenwich Village in his youth and the editor of *La Democracia* in Puerto Rico, is a poet who polishes, refines, and agonizes over nearly every word of his major speeches and articles.

Both want to build a society based not on materialism but on creativity and a better life.

The two countries have much to learn from each other. In agriculture, Israel has taken giant steps. Israel was a desert which the Jews are turning fantastically green. Puerto Rico could learn from Israel the art of large-scale industrial farming. True, in the west and on the coastal plains, Puerto Rico is doing some good mechanized farming. But in the mountains and the valleys of the interior, Puerto Rico's farmers are still farming like sharecroppers, and some of them are still peons on the land.

In 1959, Luis Rivera Santos, the Secretary of Agriculture and Commerce, attended the International Agricultural Conference in Israel and discovered the parallels that every Puerto Rican who has gone to Israel has seen. "One of the closest resemblances," he told me, "was in the spirit of the people, the decision of the people in both countries to improve their standard of living and to make their land produce."

Shortly after his return from Israel, the Secretary of Agriculture sent nine young Puerto Rican farmers to Israel to live in the co-operative and collective farms. "I sent them," the Secretary told me, "not only to train them in agriculture but also to see that other people are struggling as we are."

In industry, Puerto Rico has taken giant steps, while Israel is just beginning its big industrial push. It is only in the last few years that Israel has had the resources such as power, water, communications, and transportation, without which industry cannot function. Now Israel is studying Fomento's program, its special tax inducements, and its careful nurturing of industry, to see what can be transplanted from the Caribbean to the Mediterranean.

Fomento's boss, Ted Moscoso, visited Israel in 1959. On his return he told me, "Israel reminded me of Puerto Rico at the beginning of our revolution, the effervescence, the creativeness. They work all the time, day and night. In a week they exhausted me. They are an island surrounded by water and enemies. We, too, are an island, surrounded by water. But we are lucky. We have no enemies. It was a miracle to me to see this island of twentieth-century technology in the midst of the Middle Ages, a garden spot surrounded by desert.

"They have a lot to teach us. But what we could teach them is more reliance on private industry. They need a more aggressive industrial program. I think they could do what Britain did, not try to compete in a mass market, but to devote themselves to research and development. It's incredible what they are already doing in research in the Weizmann Institute, in the Technion and the Hebrew University. There is a great future in research. This is selling brains."

It is in the problem of migration that the two countries are completely dissimilar. Israel has two million people, Puerto Rico, one-third the size of Israel, has 2,300,000. But Israel is a land of immigration, Puerto Rico is a land of emigration. The solution of Israel's problems of defense, of security, of making the desert bloom again, lies in the people. Israel needs people and the people need the land. Puerto Rico's people must migrate to survive.

There are ties in the United States to both Puerto Rico and Israel, ties of friendship, ties of religion, ties of family and friends. But Israel has created a reservoir of good will, while Puerto Rico still remains little known and vastly misunderstood.

Now the ties between Israel and Puerto Rico are growing. On February 3, 1960, Doña Inés made the first official contribution to the Puerto Rican campaign of the United Jewish Appeal to help rescue Jews in danger abroad and bring them to Israel. "Israel and Puerto Rico have many things in common," Doña Inés said. "They do miracles there. I admire their great faith in themselves. This should be the attitude of Puerto Ricans in New York. They should be proud of themselves.

"The Puerto Rican Jewish community has always been one of

us. It has made great contributions. We are very grateful to our Jewish people on the island. Puerto Rico, like Spain, has some Jewish influence. Some of our greatest men have Jewish blood."

In the modern history of both countries, former President Harry S. Truman has played a pivotal role.

It was Truman who, brushing aside the objections of some of his close advisers, signed a document on the 14th of May, 1948, and led the world in recognizing the birth of Israel.

It was Truman who gave Puerto Rico autonomy in domestic affairs with the Elective Governor Act of 1947; a year later Muñoz became the first elected Governor of Puerto Rico in history and took office in January 1949.

"We owe a greater debt to President Truman than to any other President in American history," Dr. Arturo Morales Carrión, Puerto Rico's Under Secretary of State, told me one day in San Juan. "It's true that Roosevelt sent us Tugwell, but Truman had the first real grasp of what to do in Puerto Rico."

Truman himself considers self-government in Puerto Rico one of the most important contributions made during his administration. "What we did in Puerto Rico," he told me recently in his library in Independence, Missouri, "did more for us in Latin America, I think, than any other single thing. That's the answer for most of the world—self-government."

It was Truman who created the Point Four program in which Puerto Rico has become America's showcase of democracy. In his inaugural speech in January 1949, Truman introduced the program. It was a piece of American idealism. The United States was offering to help small nations repair their land and their people.

In San Juan and in the hills, Puerto Rico's people listened on the radio to Truman's speech. A few days later Muñoz went to see the President in Washington.

"Mr. President," he said, "we would like to become part of your Point Four program. Not to take, but to give. We're an underdeveloped country; we would like to contribute to the whole program."

He suggested that small countries could come to Puerto Rico to learn what the United States and Puerto Rico were doing together on this one island.

Governor Muñoz Marín talking with Point Four trainees

President Truman liked the idea; Muñoz was talking his language. They shook hands on a new kind of partnership.

As Muñoz left the President's conference room, the reporters swarmed around him. "What did you ask the President for?" one of the reporters asked.

Muñoz answered. "I didn't ask him for anything. I offered him something."

This was one of the turning points in Puerto Rico's history. The once sick child was no longer asking for help. It was standing straight now with self-respect and pride. It was offering something to the United States. The small countries of the world could come here and see what the United States was doing to help Puerto Rico help itself. The long night of colonial martyrdom was over.

The spark of the Point Four plan that was tried around the world took real fire in Puerto Rico. Fighting handicaps greater than in most of the underdeveloped countries of the world, the people of Puerto Rico could now show the world how they were conquering illiteracy; how they had fought for health and jobs and a decent living, developed their own political leaders, their own political ideas, their own democratic salvation, and their own capacity to solve their own problems.

President Dwight D. Eisenhower, making Puerto Rico his first stop in his good-will tour of Latin America in February 1960, suggested that other countries, striving toward self-government and economic development, had much to learn from America's free associated state in the Caribbean.

"Your program of development—rooted in self-confidence, self-help and self-achievement—has aroused tremendous interest in every area of the free world. . . . By what you have accomplished for yourselves, by the help you have given others toward a like accomplishment for themselves, you have made for the Commonwealth a record of achievement in which many other people around the globe have found hope and inspiration."

Puerto Rico's regeneration, like Israel's rebirth, has captured the imagination of small countries throughout the world. Just as Burma, Ghana, and other countries in Asia and Africa have turned to Israel to send them technicians to develop their lands, so too people from one hundred and seven different countries and territorial possessions have turned to Puerto Rico to learn of Operation Bootstrap, Operation Commonwealth, and Operation Serenity.

The visitors are chiefs of state, leading politicians, engineers, doctors, journalists, social workers, teachers—the whole spectrum of a nation's builders. They may come for a short visit, or they may stay for many months—seeing, feeling, tasting everything that Puerto Rico can teach them. They are called trainees—*becarios* in Spanish—who are selected and screened by their own countries. Most are sent to Puerto Rico by the ICA, the International Cooperation Administration of the State Department, others by the United Nations, some by the Organization of American States, private foundations, or by their own governments.

The program is directed jointly by the Technical Cooperation Administration of Puerto Rico's Department of State under Dr. Arturo Morales Carrión and by the ICA in Washington. The Government of Puerto Rico appropriates $700,000 a year toward the

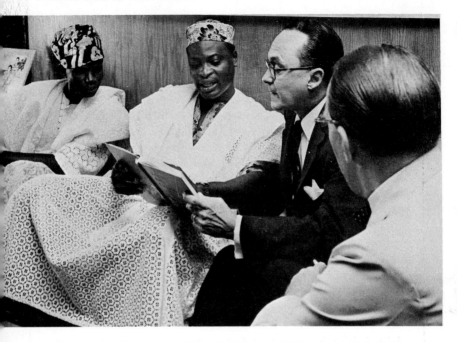

Nigerian educators, Ola Odebiye the Minister of Education and A. O. Laleye, examining a textbook with Puerto Rican educators

program; the United States, the United Nations, and other agencies contribute the rest.

All over the island it is a common sight to see lovely young women in gold and crimson saris studying a dam, African men in the colorful Ghanaian gown amusingly known in Accra as "mama," walking through the nursery in the Luis Llorens Torres housing project, or young women doctors from overpopulated India talking to Celestina Zalduondo in the Family Welfare Division, discussing the newest techniques of oral pills in controlling the exploding populations of India and Puerto Rico.

What these visitors see when they travel through the United States sometimes overwhelms them; huge projects like TVA are bigger-than-life-size for the small countries of the world. But Puerto Rico is their own size. What Puerto Rico does they can do. The

Philippines send students to study administration in municipal government. Chile, Surinam, Morocco send technicians to study housing. The Arab League, Guatemala, Costa Rica, Panama, and Colombia send special missions to study public education. Thailand sends people to study extension work in agriculture. Israel, Corsica, Yugoslavia have sent people to study the revolution in industry, and even the Soviet Ambassador, "Smiling Mike" Menshikov, went to Puerto Rico to observe the workings of the unique relationship between the United States and the Commonwealth of Puerto Rico.

"In Latin America," Antulio Rodríguez, the Director of the Office of Information of Puerto Rico's State Department, told me, "there are many people who still think of Puerto Rico as a colony. They still think the United States is an imperialist power, oppressing people with Yankee imperialism. When they come here and see our relations with the United States, and our development with the help of the United States, they have to come to the conclusion that everything that they have been told about the United States may not be true."

The greatest number of trainees comes from Latin America. "It's important when you transplant American techniques and know-how to be able to adapt them to Latin American psychology," Mr. Rodríguez said. "Latin American technicians visit Puerto Rico to see how we, as Latin Americans, have adapted American know-how. Then they can transplant what we have done in their own country. The country that sends most people here is little El Salvador. They are trying to industrialize themselves and they are already way ahead of most of the other countries. Guatemala is second, followed by Costa Rica and Honduras.

"On the islands of Trinidad, Antigua, and Jamaica, they're building $350 houses. Jamaica is putting them up especially in the sugar cane plantations; we've had a lot of visitors from Jamaica, even the governor himself. Surinam is very much interested in industrial development. They've started their own Operation Bootstrap; they call it their Ten Year Plan. They got the idea of industrialization from Puerto Rico and now Puerto Rico is their best customer, especially for plywood. Many countries come to study our methods of public administration—civil service, exams for

An Arab and an Indian, Point Four trainees, at the Trujillo Alto Dam

hiring government personnel, job security. Many take back copies of our laws and then pass them in their national legislatures, adapting them to their local psychology and social and economic needs. Some five hundred American technicians who were sent by the United States to work in Africa and other countries were flown first to Puerto Rico to see how we are solving our problems, and then sent abroad."

Not only do foreign leaders and students come to Puerto Rico to learn; Puerto Rican experts are constantly asked to go to other countries to teach. Dr. Rafael Picó, head of the Commonwealth Government Development Bank, and former president of the Planning Board, has been invited to countries in Asia and Latin America to counsel their governments in formulating long-range development programs. Experts in building dams, in health, in Fomento, in housing, in education, in political science, in labor unions, in community education, are now being invited to small countries to help them build a better life.

Puerto Rico has become an important asset in United States foreign policy. The little island has been able to establish an effortless rapport with people of all races: Indians, Indonesians, Africans, Chinese, Japanese, Hawaiians. Many who come to the island have their antenna sensitively attuned to race prejudice. In Puerto Rico they sense at once that there is no prejudice; they are accepted as human beings. Puerto Rican hospitality knows no color line. Thus they are receptive to what Puerto Rico has to teach, not only in building a dam but in building a democracy.

An African leader in Puerto Rico, Liberia's Assistant Secretary of Public Works, Charles Roberts, summed up Puerto Rico's meaning to the newly emerging nations on the African continent: "It is no wonder that Puerto Rico is making such headway and that observers like myself come here by the hundreds. The principal reason for the Commonwealth's energy is the working democracy under which every person is regarded as being important."

This is perhaps the most important contribution that Puerto Rico and Israel have to make to the nations of the world—the importance of life, the knowledge that every human being is important. Both of them are building toward a future based on peace, on human well-being, and on spiritual growth.

In the jungles of Asia and Africa, in the bazaars of the Middle East, in the remote mountains of Latin America, there are people who know Puerto Rico better than do many people living next door to Puerto Ricans in New York and Chicago.

This is our island of promise.

Hints for Travelers

More than a quarter million tourists each year now fly to Puerto Rico. It is a year-round "island paradise" where summers are barely five degrees warmer than the winters.

Men and women dress the same in Puerto Rico as in any summer resort in the States. Evenings in the mountains are cool. Puerto Ricans, in general, dress conservatively.

Since Puerto Rico is part of the United States, you don't need a passport or a visa. There is no limit on purchases you may bring back to the mainland. Puerto Rican specialties include embroidered linen dresses, embroidered blouses, pottery, mahogany bowls, paintings, sculpture, wooden Santos (religious folk art), and wrought jewelry.

American electrical appliances can be used there.

Puerto Rico has two English language newspapers: *The San Juan Star,* published daily except Sunday, and *The Island Times,* published every Friday.

For dates of special events, such as the Casals Festival, the San Juan Drama Festival, and various fishing and golf tournaments, consult any travel agency.

Information about tourism (hotels, auto rentals, guided tours), investments, and industrial and marketing opportunities, is available through the offices of the Puerto Rican Commonwealth Economic Development Administration (Fomento), 666 Fifth Avenue, New York 19, N. Y. General tourist information is available through any local travel agency.

WEATHER: The temperature range by month indicates Puerto Rico's ideal year-round climate.

	JAN.	FEB.	MAR.	APR.	MAY	JUNE	JULY	AUG.	SEPT.	OCT.	NOV.	DEC.
Low	70°	69°	70°	71°	73°	74°	75°	75°	75°	75°	73°	71°
High	80°	80°	81°	82°	84°	85°	85°	85°	86°	86°	84°	81°
Average	75°	75°	75°	77°	79°	80°	80°	81°	81°	80°	79°	76°

AIRLINES: Three airlines fly from the States to San Juan: Eastern Air Lines, Pan American World Airways, and Trans Caribbean Airways. Direct flights leave from New York, Baltimore, Washington, Chicago, Jacksonville, and Miami.

STEAMSHIPS: The Alcoa and Bull lines sail from New York; Alcoa from Baltimore and Mobile; Alcoa and Waterman lines from New Orleans; Waterman from Seattle, San Francisco, and Los Angeles; and the Lykes lines from Galveston.